BREAKING COMPROMISES II

Opportunities for Action in Consumer Markets

From the Consumer practice of

The Boston Consulting Group

This book is printed on acid-free paper. ∞

Published by The Boston Consulting Group, Inc.

ISBN: 0-9674385-1-9

Contents

Preface

Dear Reader:

We wanted you to have a complete collection of the Opportunities for Action in Consumer Markets published in 2001 and 2002. *Breaking Compromises II* follows on an earlier compilation of the articles we publish monthly for chief executives and other senior managers of large consumer companies. These articles are written by our consultants and grounded in their experiences working with many of the world's major companies. The authors provide a critical perspective on different roads to success and a continuous stream of new ideas on practical ways to improve business performance.

We are hard at work on our next book, *Trading Up: Why Americans Crave New Luxury and How Companies Create It.* Middle-market consumers are changing their purchasing patterns. They are making different choices about which goods and services are important, what constitutes quality, and what they will spend their hard-earned dollars on. As a result, they are trading both up and down. Consumers will pay a premium for the highest quality, remain loyal to those brands, and recommend them to others. But when it comes to commodities, they will look for bargains. It's the Costco phenomenon across a wide and deep palette.

Companies are responding by turning commodities into luxuries or by creating "masstige" products—affordable versions of superpremium goods. When retailers and manufacturers offer truly genuine technical, functional, and emotional benefits, they move off the old price-demand curve and achieve high profits *and* high-volume sales.

New-luxury players are supported by a significant shift in income and age demographics. Today's consumers have more disposable income, fewer children, and wealthier parents than consumers in previous generations. More women work outside the home, and role models like Oprah Winfrey encourage them to spend money on themselves. Today's consumers also change partners and jobs more frequently, and at every transition they like to "redefine" themselves with new clothes, furniture, and other personal products.

You can play in this game—but you must use a new playbook. Competition is intense, and powerful retailers are driving manufacturers to the precipice. It reminds us of a poster that Arthur Blank, former president of The Home Depot, had in his office:

> Every morning in Africa a gazelle wakes up.
> It knows it must run faster than the fastest lion or it will be killed.
> Every morning a lion wakes up.
> It knows it must outrun the slowest gazelle or it will starve to death.
> It doesn't matter whether you are a lion or a gazelle:
> When the sun comes up, you'd better be running.

The rules of time-based competition will be especially appropriate for 2003: Shrink launch and development times, respond to competitors' initiatives as if you were the leader, manage your work processes to compress non-value-added time, and understand that speed and the quality of your ideas are the new formula for success.

We believe you will find this book worth your time and energy. If you would like to discuss any of these articles in person, please e-mail one of us, and we'll put you in touch with the author.

Michael Silverstein
silverstein.michael@bcg.com

George Stalk Jr.
stalk.george@bcg.com

Michael Silverstein is a senior vice president and director in the Chicago office of The Boston Consulting Group and head of the firm's global Consumer practice. George Stalk Jr. is a senior vice president and director in the firm's Toronto office.

M-Commerce Changes the Marketing Game

Henry Elkington, Mia Kirchgaessner, and Tomas Linden

Mobile commerce will sweep across much of the Western world over the next three years, creating new opportunities to captivate the most valuable consumers. Advanced second- and third-generation broadband technologies (2.5G and 3G) will offer what has only been dreamed of: the chance to communicate with and promote products and services to individuals in all segments of a market. The promise of instantaneous one-to-one database marketing is now a reality.

That reality began over the past year with auctions for 3G mobile-phone licenses in Europe, where the bidding was far higher than expected. In the United Kingdom, offers capped out at nearly U.S.$34 billion. Bids in Germany reached $50 billion. In both countries, bidders have committed to paying more than $600 per capita just for the licenses; start-up costs and additional investments in technology are likely to be equally large. Since those auctions, the market has become disenchanted with the telecom sector, and auctions in other European countries have failed to reach the same heights. However, expectations for the potential of next-generation mobile networks remain high. Within a few years, 3G auctions are expected in the United States; their outcome is anyone's guess.

The high costs of setting up 3G mobile services have significant implications for retailers and consumer service providers. We believe that the power now residing with the companies that control the communication spectrum will shift to the companies that own customer franchises. Mobile network operators, particularly new entrants with small or nonexistent customer bases, will be under immense pressure to recoup their license and network investments. Consumer companies that can deliver large numbers of loyal customers to those operators could be in a position to negotiate favorable deals for themselves and their customers. Furthermore, these deals could go far beyond traditional cobranding and comarketing arrangements, opening up many opportunities.

Third-generation technology promises to provide a bundle of Internet-enabled mobile services—everything from instant messaging and video games to alerts and reminders—as well as myriad forms of personalized and location-specific commerce. These services represent much more than just a new channel. Depending on which forms of m-commerce consumers eventually favor, marketers could use 3G technology to extend their brands in many directions. A retailer could, for example, act as the middleman between existing customer bases and m-commerce providers. In that role, the retailer could obtain a share of the revenue stream—in the form of commissions or fees from transactions involving m-commerce goods and services—while enhancing its own customer franchise.

Banks, retailers, media companies, and even car companies could also step into the shoes of some of the weaker 3G license winners and become so-called mobile virtual-network operators (MVNOs). In that role, they would become the newest wireless players, offering competitive phone service and a free phone, which would just happen to connect directly to their own Internet portals.

There is little time to waste. Within four years, 350 million people worldwide are expected to be using the mobile Net, up from a relative handful now. That transformation will have a lasting effect on all aspects of buying and selling. As consumers begin to think differently about how they shop and make purchases, marketers will have no choice but to think differently about how they attract and retain those consumers.

The New Retail Connection

Wireless service providers make money selling "talk minutes." But as competitors have proliferated, tariffs for phone calls have plunged. Mobile data and the Internet will now be the strongest drivers of growth.

As mobile technology advances, consumers might use their wireless phones to pay for products from vending machines, locate parking spaces, call up movie reviews, check train schedules, book concert tickets, and even contact prospective mates through dating services. They will be able to send pictures and music, gamble, balance their checking accounts, and make point-of-sale purchases. A consumer in a bookstore might be able to compare the cost of buying a book at the store with the costs of ordering it online and receiving it in a few days or in an hour.

The benefits on the supply side are equally exciting. In Japan, NTT DoCoMo's i-mode service, which delivers both voice and data through a palm-sized terminal, is providing retailers with opportunities to steer customers into their stores. For example, Tsutaya, Japan's largest video-rental chain, e-mails i-mode users discount coupons, which they can redeem in video stores. During periods when the company has offered such promotions, it has seen rental fees jump nearly 60 percent and sales of nondiscounted products increase substantially as well. In the future, retailers will be able to beam real-time offers to i-mode subscribers on the basis of where they are at any moment, so that a restaurant, for example, might entice a hungry passerby.

In addition, the ability to link an e-mail address to the sender's phone number creates an opportunity for marketers to send text messages to mobile phone users while customer service representatives stand by for voice replies. And because marketers can easily access callers' buying preferences and other personal information, they can send customized advertisements and discount coupons to individuals over their cell phones.

Consider what TeleVend is doing. This small telecommunications vending company based in Israel is piloting a program with several fast-food and other retail businesses in New York to allow customers to pay for purchases using their mobile phones. Customers simply dial a number and, after a brief authentication process, the transaction is charged to their phone bill, credit card, or bank account. Once they are in the system, users can receive customized ads and discount coupons.

One of the most interesting features for retailers may be the speech recognition technology that TeleVend is developing, which will allow customers to make purchases using a "voice signature." If the technology works, the security it provides could pave the way for clerkless transactions in stores.

The ability to speed the transfer of personal data from customers to service providers will also affect the transportation industry. Delta Air Lines is already working with IBM and Modem Media, an e-commerce company, to develop and test a service that will not only give customers wireless access to flight and gate information but also allow them to purchase tickets and make flight changes using their hand-held organizers and mobile phones.

From E-Commerce to M-Commerce

As the mobile Net becomes a bigger force, how will m-commerce marketers attract and keep customers? Early data from Japan suggest that controlling portal access will be crucial. Retailers can't control portal access for personal computer users, but they could for their own mobile phone subscribers. Through their own portals, retailers could offer services provided by themselves or by others with whom they have revenue-sharing arrangements.

Retailers gain another advantage from mobile technology. Whereas online retailers have to wait for people to log on to their computers, mobile retailers will be right beside them, in their purses, briefcases, and glove compartments. And i-mode service is always on—the user doesn't have to dial in to access the Internet or to receive messages.

The most successful mobile retailers will use these advantages to add richness to their reach. Rather than simply booking a customer's plane reservations, for instance, a mobile retailer could serve the customer throughout her vacation by providing information about flights, recommending accommodations, suggesting activities and venues, finding local doctors, and helping with itinerary changes.

Some branded marketers are already leaping into the mobile business. Richard Branson, chairman of The Virgin Group, purchased idle cell-phone capacity in Britain and launched his own phone service, Virgin Mobile, in November 1999. By leveraging Virgin's brand, customer franchise, and distribution skills, Virgin Mobile has grown rapidly, gaining half a million customers in its first year.

Planning Ahead

Now is a good time—before 3G has arrived—for consumer marketers to investigate whether they might have real m-commerce opportunities. Some companies may even want to jump in with a 2.5G deal, as Virgin Mobile has, and be ready when 3G hits. Bear in mind, however, that not all of the m-commerce products and services that have been predicted will materialize. Therefore, marketers should ask themselves several questions before they commit to an m-commerce strategy:

Do our target customers have mobile phones? If they do, you can expect that those people will soon own wireless Internet-enabled personal assistants, which will provide a range of services.

Could we enhance and deepen our existing relationships with customers by offering personal mobile services linked to our core proposition? If the answer is yes, then you should play in the m-commerce space. Otherwise, you risk losing your customers to competitors with a superior proposition.

Is our brand strong enough to market a bundle of personal mobile services? If this answer is also yes, you need to consider offering your own mobile services as an MVNO. This would enable you to control the total customer proposition—as well as the customer data—and capture m-commerce commissions as the mobile portal. In particular, you should consider how becoming an MVNO could enhance your overall offline and online brand.

If you decide that there is a wireless opportunity for your company, the next steps are to develop your offering and the commercial relationship that you can bring to a mobile network operator as a partner. Without a doubt, mobile technology will elevate consumer database marketing to a new level. Although no one knows which forms of m-commerce will prove competitively sustainable, the ability to communicate and do business with individual consumers—wherever they might be, whenever they might choose—will undoubtedly pave the way for new kinds of products and services as well as new ways of marketing them. Armed with enormous customer bases and marketing savvy, retailers entering the mobile services business have the potential to become powerful forces in their newly adopted industry. The brave new world of mobile buyers and sellers is just around the corner.

This article was first published in January 2001.

Chapter Two: Revenge of the Incumbents

David Pecaut, Peter Stanger, James Vogtle, and Karen Sterling

A few years ago, it seemed that any start-up with Internet pretensions—no matter how fuzzy its business model or inexperienced its management team—could command an astonishing amount of capital. Reality emerged as the Grim Reaper in the spring of 2000, when valuations collapsed and venture capital dried up. Today the surviving e-commerce start-ups are struggling, as the old rules of business have come back with a vengeance. A market that the pundits deemed winnable by all was reclassified as winnable by none.

But that isn't the end of business-to-consumer e-commerce, only the close of Chapter One. Chapter Two is now being written, and it might be titled "Revenge of the Incumbents." Brand-name players with established reach, loyal customers, and high-quality products are now finding that they can make their move. In fact, some traditional retailers that have ventured online are discovering that their profits are larger on the Internet than in the bricks-and-mortar world. The reason: price realization and the cost of goods are the same online and offline, but the cost of online marketing and promotion can be lower than the cost of a mass-marketing television campaign or the print and postage of a direct marketing campaign. Those economics have translated into operating profits as high as 40 percent.

Such rewards will not go to those who heed the pundits' warnings, however, and cut back on existing online operations. Indeed, online revenues in most categories are continuing to grow, albeit more slowly than a couple of years ago. (See Exhibit 1.) Chapter Two's prize will be won by nimble incumbents—with strong assets—that seize the moment. That means using

Exhibit 1

Growth in the U.S. Online Retail Market Is Still Strong

Category	1998–99 online revenue growth rate (%)	1999–2000 estimated online revenue growth rate (%)
Books	110	35
Clothing and apparel	130	100
Computer hardware and peripherals	60	40
Electronics	220	170
Groceries	110	150
Health and beauty products	780	250
Music and videos	230	150
Toys	440	120
Travel services	160	105

SOURCE: *The State of Online Retailing 3.0*, a Shop.org study by The Boston Consulting Group.

real and virtual assets to provide flawless service, a complete inventory, and a well-designed site that will entice target customers to visit often.

The Demise of the Pure Plays

In 1993, $3.9 billion of venture capital was raised in the United States. By 1999, the amount had grown to $47 billion. Even larger sums will appear on the table, but pure-play online retailers will attract less of that capital than they did only a few years ago. In the early days, most venture capitalists came from the technology sector. Many backed e-commerce ventures without knowing how to evaluate a retail business or fight off competitors. Now they've gained that experience and learned from their mistakes. Today's venture capitalists want to see a compelling idea, high barriers to entry, and an experienced management team. Few pure plays can meet those demands.

Even the pure plays that have survived will have a hard time holding their places. If Chapter One was about eyeballs and revenues, Chapter Two is about cash flows and profits. Pure plays have been hard put to convince shareholders that negative cash flows will eventually become positive. The smartest ventures are scrambling to replace costly mass marketing and loss leaders with skilled direct marketers that can guarantee a profit from every new customer and a service level in line with each customer's value. Online viability will require a thorough review of cost structures, supply chains, and pricing strategies. (See Exhibit 2.)

Furthermore, the need for substantive competitive advantage is back. For a while during Chapter One, it looked as if just about anyone could attract money and launch a business. Even if one player was first with a concept, a me-too venture could still find funding. Within a few weeks in 1999, for instance, several new companies began selling pet food on the Internet. Now the land rush is over. The few successful ventures have business models that can't be duplicated easily and an offering that can be differentiated from everyone else's.

The Incumbents Return

Established companies bring a tremendous advantage to the online world: the ability to leverage their scale, distribution networks, purchasing synergies, customer relationships, and brand value. In Chapter Two, incumbents with multiple channels to consumers—and intelligent clicks-and-bricks strategies—are beginning to realize the value of their assets online. The smartest retailers are using their physical stores to attract customers to their online sites and their online sites to attract customers to their stores. The synergies created by being open for business 24 hours a day, in one channel or another, translate into more traffic, higher demand, and a larger share of a household's purchases. Not surprisingly, mail-order catalog businesses, which have experience in fulfillment and customer relationship management, have had the greatest success among the incumbents that have ventured online. (See Exhibit 3.)

Consumers can now choose how they do business with a company— whether it's through wired or wireless networks, by catalog or telephone, or in person. Furthermore, they expect to be able to move seamlessly from one channel to another, and their expectations are rising as more and more retailers begin to fulfill them. Challenging as that seamless experience is for retailers to live up to, it's an enormous opportunity to communicate brand value wherever consumers encounter the brand: on the Internet, in advertising and promotions, at the store, or through partnerships with other companies. But maintaining a consistent image across channels will be absolutely necessary to preserve customer loyalty, especially when competitors are only a click away.

Exhibit 2

Many Online Retailers Are Selling Below Direct Cost

	Computer hardware and peripherals	Clothing and apparel	Electronics
	Percentage of total revenues		
Direct costs			
• Cost of goods sold	87	53	76
• Fulfillment costs	2	17	NA
• Customer service	<1	3	4
Contribution margin before marketing costs	11	27	20
Marketing costs	6	36	35
Contribution margin after marketing costs	5	−9	−15

	Books, music, and videos	Groceries	Health and beauty products	Toys
	Percentage of total revenues			
Direct costs				
• Cost of goods sold	82	77	65	67
• Fulfillment costs	11	39	24	28
• Customer service	3	NA	6	10
Contribution margin before marketing costs	4	−16	5	−5
Marketing costs	21	17	227	220
Contribution margin after marketing costs	−17	−33	−222	−225

SOURCES: *The State of Online Retailing 3.0*, a Shop.org study by The Boston Consulting Group; BCG analysis.
NOTE: Costs do not include depreciation and overhead.

Exhibit 3

Catalog Businesses Have Gone Online Most Successfully

	Cost of goods sold	Marketing	Fulfill- ment	Customer service	Total
All online companies	76	24	10	2	112 −12
Pure plays	85	119	29	8	241 −141
Catalog businesses online	70	6	5	1	82 18
Bricks-and-mortar retailers online	82	36	22	8	148 −48

Cost as a % of revenue	Operating margin

SOURCE: *The State of Online Retailing 3.0*, a Shop.org study by The Boston Consulting Group.

Legacy Assets Reign

Chapter One was marked by stories of start-ups with practically no assets that borrowed, copied, or stole an older company's assets to launch their own businesses. Incumbents have had to learn how to exploit their assets before someone else does it for them. One major U.S. corporation, for instance, was on the verge of paying $8 million to a small e-commerce start-up to adapt its software to the company's needs. Fortunately, a manager involved in the negotiation recognized the potential benefit to the start-up of having the company as a lead customer. He reopened the negotiation, and his company ended up with a 20 percent equity stake valued at millions of dollars.

Still, it is not always easy to recognize the potential of an old asset to create new value. In Chapter Two, incumbents must look at value in terms of information and people, not just buildings and inventory. Ingram, for example, failed to realize what Amazon discovered early on: a catalog of books in inventory can be as valuable as the books themselves. One place to look for hidden assets is at concentration points in the supply chain. Ingram's warehouse operation constituted a major concentration point in book distribution because it handled a majority of all books sold in the United States. Companies that dominate their piece of the supply chain need to think about how to leverage their position to their own benefit and not someone else's.

The Imperative for Incumbents

If incumbents have the upper hand in Chapter Two, it's an advantage they must seize quickly. Competition among them for online market share promises to be intense. And over time, resourceful pure plays will build their own brands and customer relationships. For both of those reasons, the value of an incumbent's assets to an e-commerce business will never be greater than it is right now.

Being online allows a company to add value to its core business in at least four ways. First, an online channel can protect market share by helping to retain customers who prefer Internet transactions. Second, it can result in share gains over competitors that are not online, arrived online too late, or are not as proficient online, as Tesco is proving in the United Kingdom. Third, it enables the company to serve customers at a lower cost. Online transactions, for example, cost banks less than those that go through bank branches. Finally, an online channel can provide an incremental yield for the core business from such ancillary revenue streams as advertising and referral fees.

An established company can also create entirely new businesses online with tangible and intangible assets. Delta Air Lines, for example, realized that it had a valuable asset in the thousands of customers who spend hours in its terminals and planes every day—a captive market, so to speak, for such offerings as wireless services. Delta also saw an opportunity to trade assets for a stake in the New Economy by providing Priceline with distressed inventory in exchange for a share in the company. When Delta sold that stake, it was able to report a healthy addition to its balance sheet—without having invested any cash.

Succeeding Online

Incumbents have the advantage of brand value, proven experience, and a loyal customer base. But the Internet is still a very new environment, and mastering it will require effort. Here are three guidelines for incumbents to keep in mind as they cross into the new frontier:

Get the basics right. On the Internet, rivals are only a click away instead of down the block or across town. Such intense competition puts even greater pressure on Internet retailers to keep their customers happy. But giving shoppers what they want doesn't necessarily mean giving them more than they want or more than anyone else will give them. It simply means consistent performance on all of the basic aspects of online retailing: competitive prices, reliable fulfillment, secure payment processing, a large selection, and a site that is easy to use. Disappointed consumers are more likely to punish a site by never returning than delighted consumers are to reward a site with continued patronage. Therefore, a site that always delivers satisfactory service is better than one that attempts to impress with a high-wire act that works only sometimes.

Focus on customer service. Of all the aspects of online shopping, the greatest increase in dissatisfaction over the past year has been in customer service. More shoppers are contacting customer service, and more are disappointed by the results. Obviously, both the retailer and the customer lose when customer service falls short of expectations. But it goes beyond that. By providing better customer service (24-hour response, knowledgeable assistance, and alternative ways to obtain that assistance), retailers not only reap the benefit of the immediate transaction but also learn what they need to know to improve the whole shopping experience.

The standard of excellence is rising very quickly. No retailer wants to lose a customer at checkout because of technical difficulties, so many now offer both online *and* live-operator support. Consumers also want the retailer to be able to suggest purchases that are suited to their individual needs and budgets.

Provide an integrated, multichannel environment. As the Internet buzz subsides and more consumers view e-commerce as simply an additional way to shop, multichannel retailers that provide a seamless transition between channels will have a clear competitive advantage. Avoiding channel conflict is, of course, a key component of a multichannel strategy, but so is developing a consistent brand image and strong customer relationships. When there is dissonance among channels, the retailer suffers in all of them as consumers reject everything associated with the brand.

*   *   *

Well into Chapter Two, it's clear that pure plays are finding money harder to get, assets harder to borrow or steal, and profits harder to come by. Incumbents have many inherent advantages, but they must act quickly to seize the high ground. Most important will be their ability to consolidate resources, exploit legacy assets, and ensure a seamless shopping experience across channels. It's a matter of putting together what you have rather than scrambling to find what you don't. The stakes are higher—requiring more skill than luck—but so are the rewards.

This article was first published in February 2001.

Procurement: An Untapped Opportunity for Improving Profits

Steve Cobrin and Paul Gordon

Deep inside every company is a procurement opportunity that offers immediate savings, higher quality, and greatly improved profits. Taking advantage of that opportunity is one of the most critical levers a company can employ in an economic downturn. Our experience suggests that by focusing on procurement spending, companies can reduce the overall cost of materials by 5 to 10 percent. To achieve those savings, companies must develop a systematic approach to purchasing that involves aggressively managing product specifications and negotiations with suppliers. This approach also requires new capabilities and analytical skills, and a senior management team that demands improvement.

Tracking Hidden Procurement Costs

When an overheated economy cools off, manufacturers often seek efficiencies in production to reduce costs. To be sure, rationalizing production processes should be an important source of savings, but such efforts usually involve detailed process reorganization, lengthy labor negotiations, and investment in new tools and technologies—all requiring time and resources before any substantial reductions are realized. For many companies, those savings can be too little too late.

Focusing on procurement, which is usually the largest portion of a company's costs, can yield quicker and often easier savings. Yet when companies go after procurement costs, most of them either leave a lot on the table or discover that costs they thought they had eliminated have mysteriously reappeared in such forms as higher payment terms, new charges, or reduced levels of service.

One reason procurement costs get out of control is that managers don't review product specifications regularly enough to determine whether their costs are aligned with the value that is delivered to consumers or with their competitors' costs. As a result, they often miss opportunities to find less expensive materials or needlessly end up giving one supplier a monopoly on their business.

Furthermore, although most managers think they are tough at the bargaining table, few approach negotiations as rigorously as they should. As a result, cozy relationships become entrenched over the years. To combat the status quo mentality, managers need to go into negotiations armed with supplier-cost benchmarking as well as a methodical analysis of the supplier's cost structure. Managing these levers is crucial: more than 70 percent of the cost of most commodities is determined by product specifications and 30 percent by suppliers' competitiveness.

A Case of Runaway Costs

Consider the experience of a large baby-food manufacturer that had been spending close to $800 million a year on procurement. Because the company was in a high-margin business, it wasn't in the habit of monitoring procurement costs closely, and such scrutiny seemed unnecessary in a thriving economy. But as the economy started to cool and market growth slowed, the company realized that it had to make a greater effort to maintain its profit margins. Because procurement practices had not been watched carefully over the years, they were an obvious place to begin tracking hidden opportunities for savings.

The company started with its spending on MRO (maintenance, repair, and operations) supplies and quickly decided to bring in a vendor to implement an electronic-procurement strategy. That move helped reduce costs by centralizing purchases and eliminating a good deal of administrative overhead. But in the final analysis, the reductions weren't as large as the company had expected.

In search of greater savings, the company turned to its major commodities: ingredients, boxes, cans, and labels. It began by analyzing every element in its system that had an impact on procurement costs, including market forecasting, transportation, regional variations in product specifications, negotiating techniques, and relationships with suppliers. Deep into its investigation, some problems began to surface:

- The company's negotiation practices were embarrassingly ineffective. Attempts to develop an approach for identifying the strongest bargaining positions were halfhearted at best, and there was little analysis of suppliers' business economics or cost structures. As a result, procurement managers rarely challenged the status quo.

- Managers were in the habit of purchasing a variety of materials from one-stop, vertically integrated suppliers rather than finding the best supplier for each item.

- The company made little effort to compare its procurement costs with those of its competitors.

- The company lacked a mechanism for bringing the marketing and purchasing departments together on a regular basis. That meant that there was no system for assessing the costs and benefits of the materials that marketing specified.

- Finally, even when managers found opportunities for cost savings, which might require changing machine specifications or shop-floor processes, they had difficulty getting the organization to execute those changes. Any adjustments to the system took considerably longer than they should have.

Once the company realized how much it was losing by not managing its procurement spending, it launched a full-scale attack on the problem. The company prioritized its commodities, conducted a series of cost-benefit analyses, and benchmarked its costs against those of its competitors across six drivers. The effort revealed a significant cost disadvantage in materials design, the number and type of suppliers the company was using, negotiating techniques, and transportation. (See Exhibits 1 and 2.)

For example, the marketing department's specifications for packaging materials required a much thicker and more expensive paper than competitors were using, although the higher-grade paper provided no additional benefits. The company also found that the color processing of its cans involved passing over each can four times, even though a single pass would have been sufficient and obviously would have cost much less. Moreover, the

Exhibit 1

Prioritize Commodities
and Benchmark Each Cost Driver

Company A's commodities	Total cost ($millions)	Percentage of Competitors' Cost Difference		
		Materials design	Scale	Supply-base optimization
Commodity 1	133	−5.4	−0.5	−6.5
Commodity 2	219	−8.5	0.0	0.0
Commodity 3	185	−4.1	3.2	−0.6
Commodity 4	265	−3.2	0.0	−2.4
Commodity 5	265	−4.5	0.0	0.0
Weighted average		−4.4	−0.4	−1.1
Percentage of total purchases	38			

Company A's commodities	Percentage of Competitors' Cost Difference		
	Transpor-tation	Complexity manage-ment	Negotiating techniques	Total difference
Commodity 1	0.0	−2.2	0.0	−14.6
Commodity 2	0.0	−0.9	−0.5	−9.9
Commodity 3	0.0	−1.5	−1.0	−4.0
Commodity 4	0.0	−0.8	−1.8	−8.2
Commodity 5	−0.9	−1.5	0.0	−6.9
Weighted average	−0.4	−1.1	−1.0	−8.4

SOURCE: BCG analysis.

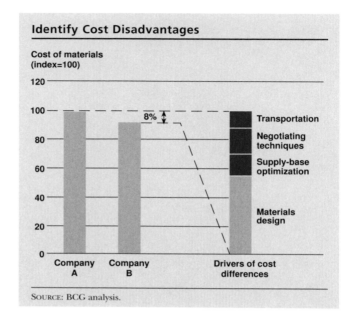

company was using two labels (front and back) on its less valuable brands when one would have been adequate. And finally, because of multiple brands and SKUs, the timing of regional promotions, and different content configurations for labels in different regions, the company's labels were being printed in short runs rather than less expensive long runs. In fact, as many as 80 percent of the company's labels were produced in short runs, while its major competitor printed 80 percent of its labels in long runs.

Because the company didn't have a system to monitor the costs and benefits of specifications, managers had failed to realize that they did not necessarily need materials that were so expensive or involved costly processes. Once it had identified prospects for cost reduction in its specifications, the company then moved to bring the marketing, sales, and production people together regularly so that it could continue to seize those opportunities over the long term.

The next task was to develop a set of aggressive negotiating practices. This required a detailed cost and capability assessment of current and potential suppliers, including an analysis of suppliers' cost structures.

For example, the company discovered that it was using the highest-priced supplier for one of its major ingredients. When it analyzed that supplier's cost structure, it found that the supplier was in fact pricing as low as it could considering its own relatively high costs. The company then researched other suppliers' cost structures—complex detective work that took into account the location of farms and refining facilities, the costs of electricity and labor, and the size of plants, among other factors. It discovered several suppliers whose cost structures put them in a better position to offer lower prices.

The company also looked more closely at one of its one-stop suppliers, which not only supplied boxes but also sourced the paper for the boxes and had it printed. After researching other paper and print suppliers' costs, the company realized that it could buy the paper and have it printed for less than the box supplier was charging. When the company pointed this out in negotiations, the supplier was forced to lower its price or lose the company's business. Deconstructing the vertical supply chain to reveal discrete costs turned out to be a valuable negotiating lever.

As a result of these efforts, the company saved 12 percent of the value-added portion of its materials costs. The savings were split evenly between improved product specifications and smarter negotiating techniques.

A Strategic Approach to Procurement Costs

To rein in runaway procurement costs, companies need an overall procurement strategy that includes optimized specifications and tough supplier negotiations. (See Exhibit 3.) To support those objectives, companies must

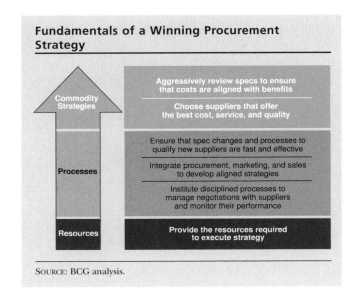

Exhibit 3   **Fundamentals of a Winning Procurement Strategy**

SOURCE: BCG analysis.

establish two continuous processes. The first is regular, comprehensive reviews of the costs and benefits of product specifications, including a breakdown of competitors' products. The reviews should be coupled with a system for integrating procurement, marketing, sales, and production to align strategies and ensure that decisions on specification changes are quickly implemented.

The second process that is essential to a procurement strategy is one for managing negotiations on the basis of an analysis of suppliers' cost structures and performance. In following such a process, managers must

- identify the issues to be addressed in negotiations

- determine objectives for cost reduction and improvements in quality and service levels

- define points of leverage and a credible switching strategy

- choose a negotiating strategy based on the costs of switching, the number of suppliers, and the company's confidence in its price reduction targets

- develop a step-by-step plan for negotiations, specifying when senior management should be involved

- ensure suppliers' continual improvement by monitoring their performance at clearly established checkpoints

To determine whether your company's procurement costs are as low as they can go, and to ensure that your negotiations with suppliers are as tough as they can be, ask your organization these questions:

- When was the last time we looked at alternative sources for our most important commodities? When was the last time we switched suppliers?

- Are our specifications consistent with the value they provide to consumers? Do they needlessly constrain the breadth of the supply base?

- Do we understand the cost structures, cost drivers, and profit margins of our key suppliers? Do we know how much they make by serving us? Do we know how important we are to them?

- Are our suppliers motivated to work with us to reduce costs?

In procurement, knowledge is power. Over and over again, we have found that a thorough assessment of product specifications and an accurate understanding of suppliers' cost structures can yield substantial savings in negotiations. With the prices of many raw materials rising and the economy in flux, now is a good time for consumer goods companies to get aggressive in their focus on procurement costs.

This article was first published in March 2001.

Consumer Services: The Master Brands of the Twenty-First Century

Brad Banducci and Ben Keneally

For many years, consumer service brands were considered the poor cousins of product brands. Services were often undifferentiated and claimed little brand equity in consumers' minds. Choosing a brand meant deciding between Huggies and Pampers, Folgers and Maxwell House. Packaged-goods brands ruled.

No longer. Today the most exciting stories in branding are coming out of the service sector. Almost all new blockbuster brands, like Dell and Starbucks, are primarily service oriented. E-commerce is creating instant service brands such as eBay, Amazon, and Yahoo! And the service environment in which we shop has itself become a brand: before we choose a brand of diapers or coffee, we decide whether to make those purchases at a Tesco supermarket, a Carrefour hypermarket, or a Wal-Mart supercenter. Service brands are also starting to go global. Witness the recent cross-border growth of Carrefour and Wal-Mart, consumer banks Citibank and HSBC, and mobile phone companies Vodafone and Orange.

The enthusiasm for service brands has shown up in other ways as well. Over the past ten years, the market capitalization of consumer service companies in the United States has grown considerably faster than that of consumer product and retail companies. And spending on advertising for service brands has increased at a rate that is more than five times higher than that for product brands. (See Exhibits 1 and 2.)

The rise of service brands presents new challenges for providers of services and products alike. Service providers face mounting competition as a

Exhibit 1   **The Market Value of U.S. Consumer-Service**
                 Companies Has Soared

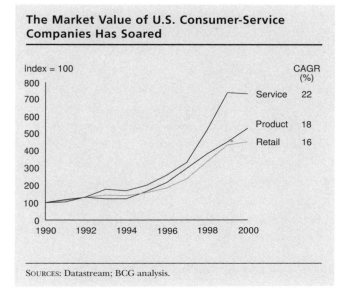

SOURCES: Datastream; BCG analysis.

Exhibit 2   **U.S. Consumer-Service Companies**
                 Spend Heavily on Advertising

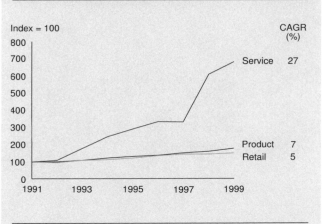

SOURCE: *Advertising Age.*
NOTE: Owing to the mix of businesses, AOL Time Warner and IBM are
not included.

result of deregulation, e-commerce, and globalization—not to mention growing pressure from shareholders to deliver on the sector's increasing valuation. For their part, product marketers are under intense pressure from assertive service providers, who are using their strength to demand large concessions for retail support or for placement in the service environment. As a result, some product marketers are beginning to experiment by offering services over the Internet to reach consumers directly.

Given this increasing competition, all marketers need to pay close attention to what the best service companies are doing today. In essence, these companies are creating *master brands*—trusted names that signify a rewarding experience and can extend across many consumer categories. Their recent success offers important lessons in capturing the inherent advantages of service brands.

The Service Brand Advantage

Service brands have a potentially powerful advantage over product brands. Why? Because a service is an *action*, performed over and over again *with* the consumer, whereas a product is a *thing* that is given *to* the consumer, usually without his or her involvement in the production process. From that broad distinction, several other important differences follow. (See Exhibit 3.)

Exhibit 3

Services Versus Products

A service is an *action*		A product is a *thing*
Services cannot be stored	⟺	Products can be stored
Production and consumption occur simultaneously	⟺	Production and consumption can be separated
The consumer is often involved in the production process	⟺	The consumer tends not to be involved in the production process
Services are usually consumed in the provider's environment	⟺	Products are consumed wherever the consumer wants
Service consumption is often continuous	⟺	Product consumption is usually discrete

Source: BCG analysis.

These differences add up to the potential for more frequent and complex interactions between the service provider and the customer, and thus more opportunities for the service provider to create a positive impression. The corollary, of course, is that there are also more opportunities for the service provider to create a negative impression.

Just think about your most recent international flight. You probably

- paid a premium for a flexible ticket

- had contact with many airline employees in a series of environments, including the check-in counter, the frequent-flier lounge, the boarding gate, and the plane itself

- received your preferred seating and meal choice

- read the in-flight magazine and watched the in-flight program

- purchased some duty-free items

In all, you spent several hours with the brand and probably came away with a lasting positive or negative impression. A lot is at stake for the airline every time you travel. If your impression is positive, the airline not only will retain a particularly profitable customer but also might get an unpaid ambassador of goodwill.

The opportunity for an airline or other service provider to create such strong brand equity is founded on four advantages that flow from the service interaction.

Time with the Consumer. Every moment that a consumer spends directly or indirectly with a brand—whether it is time flying on a plane, paying a bill, or dealing with a service agent—is an opportunity to reinforce the brand's value.

Rich, Personal Connections. The brand environment and the people who staff it can influence consumers directly and personally. Unlike advertising, effective brand environments appeal to all of the senses, and a good staff can respond to an individual's needs.

Advantaged Information. Successful branders use the customer information their services generate to improve the brand experience and support personal marketing initiatives. Even such services as utilities, which do not involve much personal interaction, know more about their customers (addresses, usage patterns, profitability) than do many product businesses.

The Segmentation Multiplier. Not only are service businesses in a better position to segment customers on the basis of information about them, but also the rewards that flow from such segmentation can be greater than they are for product businesses. Because services tend to be more perishable—yesterday's airline ticket is no good today—and costs are generally fixed, customer profitability varies more in services than in product businesses. And because service providers know which customers are most profitable, they can devote resources to attracting them.

Developing the Service Advantage

The best service brands are beginning to make the most of their advantages by developing three capabilities. First, they are aligning their processes, organizational structures, and environments to deliver a consistently superior brand experience. Second, they are harnessing the power of customer information to enhance the experience. Third, they are leveraging that information to expand their offerings into additional categories. Here is a six-step process that master branders follow to build those capabilities:

Take responsibility for the entire service experience. When receiving a service, a customer may come in contact with many different parts of an organization. Mapping those points of contact, analyzing the value that is delivered, and orchestrating all the connections in between provide the basis for a consistent and highly differentiated experience. Delivering that experience requires taking brand management beyond the traditional marketing functions into such areas as human resources, property management, information systems, and customer service itself. In fact, the most successful service brands place responsibility for those functions at the highest levels of the organization.

Make sure that facilities and employees amplify the brand's values. The brand environment—whether it is a store, an airplane, or a Web site—and the people who staff it determine how well a brand lives up to its promise. A well-designed environment can facilitate service delivery and provide important visual cues for the brand's values. McDonald's, for instance, is famous for its detailed instructions on store cleanliness and its processes for ensuring that employees follow those instructions—all of which reinforce the brand's family-oriented image. Recruitment and training initiatives, rewards programs, and monitoring and measuring systems are designed to make sure that employees subscribe to and consistently communicate the brand's values.

Build in the flexibility to manage "moments of truth." Each contact with a consumer is an opportunity for a brand to make—or break—its promise. But some interactions are more important than others—either because problems have previously occurred at those points or because great value is on the line, as when a customer files an insurance claim for the first time. Companies should look closely at all contact points and note which might be the most sensitive. Then they should make sure that their service format, information systems, and staff policies are flexible enough to let employees handle those moments smoothly. Service recovery can be as important as service perfection.

Use information about consumers to improve the service experience. Leading service brands use up-to-the-minute information not only to personalize each customer's experience but also to tailor the service, making it less expensive and more relevant and enjoyable. They might even use such information to develop more attractive products. Powerful brands have systems to help them learn about their customers, and they use that information to improve their offerings. As a result, their customers become increasingly loyal as the service distinguishes itself from that of competitors. A successful supermarket chain, for example, uses information about the purchasing behavior of its customers to refine its individualized mailings and help determine the products and brands each store carries.

Aspiring service brands should note, however, that although many companies have invested in databases for customer relationship marketing, few have fully exploited them. Gathering data is only the first step: the payoff comes from using the data to create the right kind of service experience.

Develop segmented branding strategies. Given the wide range of customer profitability in services and the availability of detailed information, the most successful service brands have come to understand the art of acquiring and serving the best customers while maintaining good relationships with the rest. They understand the key levers for increasing a customer's profitability—such as cross-selling, up-selling, reducing churn, increasing transaction size, and enhancing channel usage—and they design segmented strategies to manipulate those levers. They invest selectively and profitably in the elements of the service that matter most to high-value customers.

Use the service advantage to move into new categories. Powerful service brands are increasingly able to monetize their contact with customers by expanding their offerings into new categories. Virgin is no longer an anomaly. Indeed, many service providers are now capable of leveraging the information they collect, the location of distribution facilities, and relationships with their current customers to create competitive advantage in new businesses. Leading grocery retailers such as Tesco and Sainsbury's, for example, are branching out into gasoline retailing, financial services, and mobile telephony. The trick is to identify the needs of a category's consumers, determine the sources of competitive advantage in meeting their needs, and then develop an offering that is consistent with the service brand's core values.

*   *   *

The imperative for all brands—service and product alike—is to deliver a compelling experience. The service interaction is increasingly important for achieving that goal. Service providers have a natural advantage, and some are on their way to becoming true master brands: highly trusted signifiers of quality, value, and emotional connection across a variety of products and services.

Product marketers should also strive for a stake in the service interaction. Direct sales, assisted by the Internet and wireless technology, will offer product companies many more opportunities to deal directly with consumers and thus incorporate service interactions into their offerings. As for service providers that have yet to capture the full value of the service interaction, the gauntlet has been thrown down. Why not make your brand one of the master brands of the twenty-first century?

This article was first published in April 2001.

Keeping the Promise: How Big Brands Can Win Online

Rob Lachenauer, David E. Williams, and Berenice Mariscal

Although most major consumer brands have established some kind of presence on the Internet, only a handful have transferred their brand experience online with any success. Fewer than half of the 60 most visited Internet sites, as tracked by Media Metrix, represent incumbent brands. And of those incumbents, only three—Disney, Microsoft, and Sony—are in the top 60 of Interbrand's list of worldwide brands.

The Boston Consulting Group studied more than 80 online retail brands that Media Metrix and others identify as having frequently visited sites. BCG found that despite the large volume of visitors, nearly four-fifths of the sites have neither differentiated themselves from their online competitors nor improved the online brand experience. The primary reason for this lackluster performance seems to be a lack of understanding of what is required to extend a brand online. As consumers grow increasingly comfortable moving between offline and online markets, companies with powerful legacy brands will miss a tremendous opportunity if they fail to exploit the Internet's ability to enrich the brand promise, increase customer loyalty, and attract new sources of revenue.

Taking the Brand Promise Online

Great brands become great by establishing and keeping a set of promises that consumers understand, appreciate, and trust. In fact, when they navigate the Web's limitless options, consumers depend on well-known brands even more than they do offline. By transferring the experience of a trusted brand to an Internet site, a company can enhance the brand and increase its differentiation.

Consider Southwest Airlines. The company's renowned promise of point-to-point routing, inexpensive fares, and customer-friendly policies is reinforced online with a straightforward search-and-purchase process. On Southwest's site, customers can call up flight schedules and prices in one step, and conclude a purchase with just four more clicks. In fact, a traveler can buy a ticket on southwest.com in less than two minutes—more than a minute (a veritable eternity on the Internet) less than it takes to complete the same transaction on most competitors' sites. The results are telling: by the end of June 2000, 31 percent of Southwest's passenger revenues came from bookings on its Web site, compared with the 2.5 percent of revenues that the two largest U.S. carriers received from their sites.

To earn customer loyalty in the face of intense competition, a company must deliver on its brand promise and do so in a way that is truly engaging. The issue for companies on the Internet then becomes how best to captivate the online consumer. Like Southwest, the most successful brands translate their promise to the Internet in at least one of three ways:

- They re-create the best parts of the in-store experience, including the services of a great salesperson or agent

- They reach targeted consumers by providing informative, engaging entertainment that reflects the brand promise

- They establish a supportive community of customers with common interests and provide links to other users

The Online Salesperson

Online retailers and service providers are beginning to replicate the in-store brand experience by providing consumers with opportunities for continuous feedback and two-way communication. Like a good offline sales staff, virtual salespeople inspire trust, understand customers' needs, and find solutions to problems. They streamline processes, close deals, and keep promises concerning quality, delivery, and timeliness. Virtual salespeople offer an interactive, personal approach rather than a purely transactional one.

Lands' End, for example, has created a virtual salesperson in its My Personal Shopper feature, which encourages consumers to compare styles, colors, patterns, and fabrics. The online salesperson then helps them make selections that match their individual tastes. Because the retailer understands that shoppers are more likely to buy when they have a friend along to encourage them, the site's Shop with a Friend feature allows two people in different locations anywhere in the world to navigate the site together, look at the same screen, and discuss the options.

Shoppers can also "try on" outfits by filling out a questionnaire about their measurements and body types, then seeing the outfit they select displayed on a model who resembles themselves or a famous person. Unlike most of its competitors, which offer little more than special-occasion reminders and address lists for gifts, the Lands' End site is a true extension of the brand promise that customers have come to expect from the company's catalog and outlet stores.

Best Buy is another company that is outpacing its rivals online. Although Amazon carries a line of electronics similar to that offered by Best Buy, the latter's site gives consumers a richer experience by offering them the kind of assistance they receive in the company's offline stores. For instance, both sites allow shoppers to compare products, but Best Buy helps them navigate the shopping experience more effectively with Shopping Assistant, a service that helps narrow the range of selections on the basis of features the customer values. That service, coupled with increasingly detailed levels of information (which let customers learn as much as they want about a product and its features), sets Best Buy apart from Amazon. And once a shopper has decided to make a purchase, Best Buy's virtual salesperson suggests complementary items that are keyed to the personal information the customer has provided. In this way, it replicates the efforts of a skilled salesperson, who knows how to cross-sell and up-sell in a way that doesn't feel like a canned pitch.

Other incumbent brands that have re-created a great online salesperson include FordDirect, which allows customers to specify the exact vehicle they want, and Tesco, the British grocery chain whose Web site offers detailed product information and vast cross-category selection. Companies that go to the trouble to provide consumers with information and offers that correspond to their needs understand that people often buy more products—and more expensive ones—on the basis of well-presented information. Personalized information directs consumers to the right products, and personal interaction closes the deal.

Let Us Entertain You

Some companies with legacy brands have discovered that entertainment on the Web can help position their brands and increase sales by providing a compelling environment in which the companies can interact directly with targeted consumers. Of course, a company whose products are entertainment—such as Sony—can integrate entertainment with the sales process so that product awareness arises naturally. Visitors to sony.com can post questions or comments about favorite PlayStation video games, send a Musicgram that features a Sony artist, or read about what people all over the world are listening to on their Walkman players. Such activities leverage Sony's products and, not so incidentally, show visitors what they may be missing.

But even companies that aren't directly involved in entertainment or don't sell their products online have found entertaining ways to communicate their brand experience on the Internet. The Nike brand, for example, has long stood for excellence as well as the quest for excellence. Nike.com reinforces both themes by letting visitors chat with world-famous soccer players or download music from up-and-coming artists. In a similar way, Pepsi has translated its "new generation" theme online with youth-oriented sports and arcade games, as well as music by popular artists. In a recent promotional campaign, Pepsi gave offline customers points on purchases, which they could redeem on Pepsistuff.com for items such as video games, fleece jackets, and CD mixes.

By harnessing the Internet's interactivity and mixed media (picture, video, and voice), brands not directly associated with entertainment can benefit from the power of entertainment to attract consumers to a site where, over time, they will come to associate the brand with a positive experience.

Create a Community of Interests

Consumers, especially young ones, like to congregate and affiliate on the basis of shared ideals, goals, and concerns. Relationships founded on affinity and common interests are powerful catalysts for creating communities of loyal online customers. Petsmart is a good example of a company that has established an online community based on a strong emotional bond—the deep feelings that people have for their pets. Animal lovers can talk with each other in one of eight chat rooms, post messages on dozens of message boards, and search shelters to find pets to adopt. They can design their own

Web pages and, once a week, log on to discuss their pets' health with a veterinarian.

Security issues, however, continue to be the leading inhibitors of online communities. Visitors need assurances and compelling benefits to overcome these concerns. A few online brands, such as eBay, have been unusually successful in developing secure, content-rich online communities. To accomplish that feat, the company builds trust among its members by requiring them to use just one online identity. Members know that their e-mail addresses won't be given out without their permission. But because they have a traceable online identity, they also know that they will be held accountable for their actions. The site tracks individuals' behavior, provides facilitators and experts, and continues to make improvements on the basis of comments posted by visitors to the site.

An online community can be a powerful tool for transmitting brand value, but it can also be a two-edged sword. On the one hand, communities can attract attention to products that have been underrated. On the other, they can bring undesirable exposure to products that are failing to live up to their brand promise. To build an online community that reinforces the brand, managers should maintain the following standards:

Brand Strength. The brand should be strong enough to maintain its positive image even if the community presents negative views about some of its products.

Privacy Protection. Users should feel certain that their privacy will be respected and that confidential information will not be revealed to a third party without their permission.

Targeted Audience. The site should attract users of the site sponsor's products. It makes no sense to establish a community that doesn't promote sales.

Emotional Connection. The community should have a strong emotional component that cements members' attraction to the brand and to one another, and encourages them to share information.

*   *   *

The rules for transferring a valuable brand experience online are becoming clearer. The most successful sites have replicated their offline environments with skilled virtual salespeople, entertainment targeted to the most desirable consumers, and communities that attract loyal customers. The right mix of those components—fulfillment, entertainment, and community—will do more to enhance a brand, both offline and online, than any amount of advertising.

Established brands have a natural advantage on the Internet because online consumers gravitate to names they recognize and trust. But so far, relatively few incumbents have exploited their advantage fully. One thing is absolutely clear by now: just putting in an appearance on the Internet isn't enough. The key is to provide an all-encompassing experience. Focusing on discrete components of brand building—Web site design, positioning, advertising, packaging, logos, and slogans—is futile without an understanding that the total experience is greater than the sum of its parts. Furthermore, online behavior is hyperkinetic: BCG's study of more than 12,000 online consumers indicates that people "channel surf" three times as frequently on the Internet as they do when they watch television. A Web site has only 60 seconds to sell itself before the consumer moves on.

Incumbents do have an advantage online, but it is transitory: if they don't use it, they lose it. The typical online consumer gives a new site only one or two chances. After that, it becomes a bookmark or dies. As soon as you put this article down, go online and check out your site and those of your competitors. Which has the best salespeople? The best entertainment? The best community?

This article was first published in May 2001.

Winning the Online Consumer:
The Challenge of Raised Expectations

Nina Abdelmessih, Michael Silverstein, and Peter Stanger

Despite the recent demise of a number of dot-com sites and some dire predictions about the future of e-commerce, consumers' enthusiasm for online shopping is rising. The notion that e-commerce is fading away is based not on consumer activity but on business failures: many Web-based companies built their infrastructures ahead of demand and adopted unrealistic economic forecasts.

In the second of a series of reports focusing on consumer behavior in the online environment, The Boston Consulting Group found that consumers are more passionate about the Internet than ever before—because it is convenient, because it provides access to vast selection, and because it saves time.[1] BCG's research shows that online purchases in North America totaled $45 billion last year—up from $27 billion in 1999. For 2001, we are forecasting still another jump, to $65 billion.

On the business side, Web-based retailers are being swept aside by incumbents. The legacy player with a brand, an established customer base, a broad product offering, and a strong fulfillment capability is going to be hard to beat.

---

1. This OfA has been adapted from *Winning the Online Consumer 2.0: Converting Traffic into Profitable Relationships,* February 2001. The findings of the report were based on comprehensive surveys of 2,876 U.S. Internet purchasers during the fourth quarter of 2000. The surveys were augmented by quantitative research derived from one-on-one interviews and the *Harris Interactive e.commercePulse Q2 2000 Database,* a study tracking the online and offline shopping and purchasing behavior of approximately 100,000 online consumers.

But while consumers are spending more on the Internet, they are also demanding more from those who are doing the selling. They are becoming increasingly intolerant of slow downloads, inconvenient navigation, limited selection, and checkout failure. Online retailers must produce an experience that is as good as or better than the familiar one of shopping in a bricks-and-mortar store. Though incumbents have the edge, many online retailers are not making the most of their opportunities, and one of the reasons is their inability to meet consumers' rising expectations.

Eager Consumers, Dissatisfied Customers

Online expectations are higher for several reasons. For one, the media have hyped online shopping as cheaper and easier than offline shopping could ever be. For another, consumers have become more proficient at using the Internet, and they expect no less of the retailers they do business with. Yet another reason is that the novelty of online shopping has worn off. More and more consumers go online not simply to be entertained or to see what's there but to get things done. The honeymoon is over.

Complaints about all aspects of the online shopping experience—from navigation to delivery—have become much more widespread, according to the new BCG survey. Almost 70 percent of online consumers reported that some Web sites take too long to download, and more than half said that a site crashed before they could complete a purchase, compared with 56 percent and 32 percent, respectively, in 1999. What is worse, as many as 20 percent of online consumers had difficulty getting a site to accept their credit cards, up from only 12 percent the year before—a disturbing development for people who are already uneasy about releasing credit card information online. Moreover, as many as 11 percent of consumers had at some time ordered and paid for products that they never received, compared with 6 percent in 1999.

Retailers cannot afford to ignore these statistics, because consumers are increasingly likely to act on their disappointment. Some 60 percent of those polled in the new study changed their online behavior as a result of a failed purchase attempt, compared with fewer than 54 percent of those surveyed in 1999. The impact on individual retailers is particularly harsh, as consumers are increasingly inclined to punish offending sites rather than blame the Internet as a channel. (See Exhibit 1.)

Exhibit 1

Consumers Blame the Site, Not the Channel

Percentage of consumers experiencing purchase failures who agree

	1999	2000
I stopped shopping online	6	2
I stopped purchasing online	10	2
I stopped shopping at that particular Web site	28	41
I stopped purchasing at that particular Web site	23	30
I stopped shopping at that particular company's offline stores	6	9

SOURCES: *BCG Q4 2000 Online Purchaser Survey; BCG Q4 1999 Proprietary Consumer Database* (N = 948 for 2000; N = 376 for 1999).

The Benefits of Satisfaction: Loyalty and Share Gain

Consumers' impatience with less-than-satisfactory purchase experiences ought to be reason enough to intensify the focus on customer satisfaction. But there is an even greater incentive for doing so, one that bears directly on the bottom line.

Our research shows that satisfied online customers shop more, spend more, and buy more frequently and across more categories. A satisfied customer is more likely to return to a Web site for additional purchases and, equally important, to recommend the site to others. Our study found an almost perfect correlation between a site's overall satisfaction ratings and the likelihood that a customer would recommend that site. (See Exhibit 2.) The positive impact of satisfied customers—and the negative impact of dissatisfied ones—have a greater compounding effect on the bottom line than most retailers realize.

Increased loyalty and advocacy are two of the most valuable results of improved customer satisfaction. Loyal, satisfied customers buy more during each visit and visit more often, and the combined effect of higher purchasing frequency and larger average orders is that satisfied customers spend 57 percent more than dissatisfied ones. Thus, satisfied customers amortize the high cost of customer acquisition and become profitable more quickly.

Satisfaction Drives Loyalty and Advocacy

Average likelihood to repurchase or recommend

Repurchase

Recommend

Overall satisfaction rating of Web site

SOURCES: *Harris Interactive e.commercePulse Q2 2000 Database* (based on 30,923 responses); BCG analysis.

Advocacy, the ultimate form of loyalty, contributes at least three additional benefits: lower customer-acquisition costs, of course, but also lower customer-retention costs and higher customer-conversion rates (the number of buyers divided by the number of unique visitors to a site). Advocacy improves customer retention by reinforcing a positive picture of the retailer in the mind of the customer who makes the recommendation. Moreover, people who visit a site because it was recommended to them are much more likely to buy something from it than shoppers attracted by conventional marketing techniques.

The Profit Driver Framework illustrates how customer satisfaction metrics relate to the operating profitability of online retailers. (See Exhibit 3.) It separates revenues and operating costs into their component parts and highlights the wide range of drivers most affected by customer satisfaction. In fact, satisfying customers at every stage of the buying process can have a combined effect large enough to push the average online retailer into the black.

Exhibit 4 illustrates how realistic performance improvements at a hypothetical average online clothing retailer could move the company from an operating loss of 78 percent of revenue to an operating profit of 7 percent. Such results do not assume best-in-class performance on any one dimension.

Consider the top 10 percent of retailers, which achieve customer conversion rates higher than 9 percent and 67 percent of whose sales are to repeat customers. That level of conversion and loyalty performance would produce an operating profit of 14 percent of revenue in our model.

Retailers should note, however, that success depends on improving performance on all dimensions at the same time. Increasing the number of unique visitors or the proportion of repeat customers will improve results, but no single lever will put profitability within reach. (See Exhibit 5.)

Finally, what is happening in e-commerce is an old story, and its moral—one that catalogers have known for years—is about acquiring and serving the right customers. Mail-order retailers call it RFM (recency, frequency, monetary value)—a straightforward, data-driven formula that lets them segment their customer base and focus on the high rollers. Catalogers know they will succeed if they focus on their best customers: the most recent, the most frequent, and the biggest spenders. Online retailers that monitor RFM as catalogers do will greatly increase their odds of survival.

Meeting Expectations

The message is clear: The quality of the purchase experience matters. Retailers that have Web sites or are considering such a venture should pay close attention to the following critical elements of a flawless online performance:

Site and Brand Awareness. In the rush to go online, retailers sometimes neglect the basic rule of marketing: Know who your potential customers are and create messages geared to them. Multichannel retailers also need to make sure that the message and the customer experience are consistent across channels. At its best, the branding in each channel will reinforce the overall brand.

Site Navigation. A Web site should tailor its features to the user's needs. This means not only personalization—now virtually a requirement—but also a recognition that different consumers use different modes of access, have different connection speeds, and employ different software and plug-ins. Sites may also need to include entertainment to make them more than a catalog of products.

Product Offering and Selection. A good Web site's offering must be comprehensive and let visitors compare products. Shoppers need a clear presentation of prices, taxes, and shipping costs before they begin the checkout process. Inventory status should be clearly indicated at the time of the search, not after the customer has placed the order. Clicks-and-bricks retailers can go one step further and integrate their inventory systems, allowing shoppers to check a product's availability both online and at the local store.

Ordering. The ordering process should be intuitive. It must also guarantee—and demonstrate—a high level of security and privacy. Sites should have an express-checkout option that reduces the number of screens and the amount of data customers must enter. Once customers place an order, they should receive confirmation and information about order tracking.

Delivery. Delivery should be reliable and consistent with the retailer's economics and brand positioning. It makes no economic sense to offer

Exhibit 3   **The Profit Driver Framework: Satisfied Customers Improve Key Elements of Online Retailers' Economics**

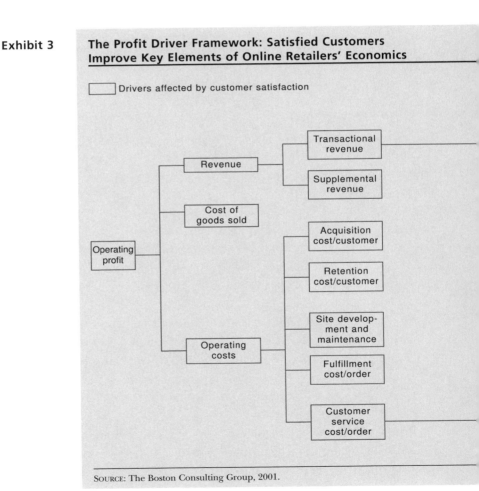

SOURCE: The Boston Consulting Group, 2001.

overnight delivery, for instance, when customers are content to wait two or three days.

Customer Service. Of all the aspects of online shopping we surveyed, the one that provoked the greatest increase in dissatisfaction was customer service. By dealing with potential problems and providing a truly self-serve environment, retailers can minimize customers' need for assistance. The basic requirements of customer service are multichannel contact (phone, e-mail, fax) and 24/7 response.

Returns. Returns remain a major concern for online consumers, and few retailers have responded to their calls for a smoother process. Many customers would prefer to make returns at a local store, but for most online

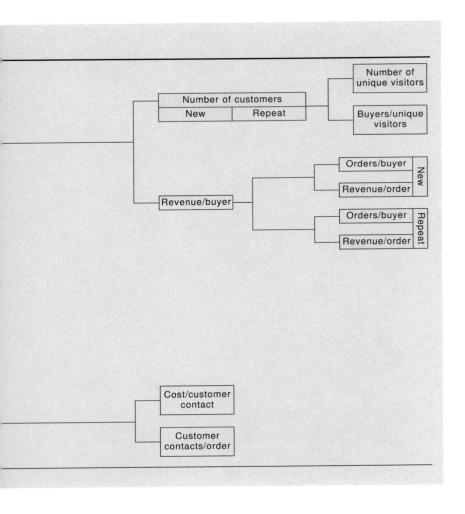

Exhibit 4

Satisfying Customers Can Significantly Affect the Bottom Line

Hypothetical Online Clothing Retailer

Satisfaction levers	Average online retailer	Online retailer that satisfies
Conversion rate (buyers/unique visitors)	1.8%	4%
Unique visitors (index to 100)	100	125
Proportion of repeat customers	21%	35%
Number of orders per year/customer	2	3
Ratio of repeat-order revenue to first-time-order revenue	120%	150%
Operating profit/loss as % of revenue	−78%	7%

Profitability is within reach for the typical retailer.

SOURCES: *The State of Online Retailing 3.0* (a Shop.org study by The Boston Consulting Group), performance benchmarks; BCG analysis.

Exhibit 5

It Takes More Than One Lever to Reach Profitability

Hypothetical Online Clothing Retailer

Satisfaction levers	Average online retailer	Impact of a single lever on operating profitability				
Conversion rate (buyers/unique visitors)	1.8%	(4.0%)	1.8%	1.8%	1.8%	1.8%
Unique visitors (index to 100)	100	100	(125)	100	100	100
Proportion of repeat customers	21%	21%	21%	(35%)	21%	21%
Number of orders per year/customer	2	2	2	2	(3)	2
Ratio of repeat-order revenue to first-time-order revenue	120%	120%	120%	120%	120%	(150%)
Operating profit/loss as % of revenue	−78%	−21%	−62%	−65%	−61%	−67%

SOURCE: BCG analysis.

retailers, this option is still prohibitively expensive. Retailers that can figure out how to meet this demand cost-effectively could gain a significant competitive advantage.

*   *   *

Giving online consumers what they want doesn't have to involve giving them more than they want or even more than anyone else will give them. It simply means performing consistently on all the essential elements of online retailing. Up to now, most retailers have focused on building awareness of their sites and bringing traffic to them. Meanwhile, consumers have been so taken with the novelty of the Internet that they have been willing to keep trying when a transaction didn't go as smoothly as they had expected. That environment has lured many retailers into believing that an online presence was enough.

Now that the grace period is over, what counts is the quality of the day-to-day experience. Retailers that meet the challenge of consumers' rising expectations will create a virtuous cycle of higher purchase and conversion rates, increased loyalty, and greater advocacy—all of which will substantially enhance the brand and improve the bottom line. Pure plays and legacy players that fail to adapt will be left behind.

Internet retailing is quickly becoming both an art and a science. Applying advanced direct-marketing analysis and creating a superior consumer experience are a sure formula for results.

This article was first published in June 2001.

The Antidote to Mismanaged CRM Initiatives

Carlos Costa, Christophe Duthoit, Nicholas Keuper,
Kate Sayre, and Miki Tsusaka

Most companies don't know who their best customers are. They enjoy the profits that accrue from those customers, but they don't take full advantage of the information generated in the transactions. Customer relationship management (CRM) can remedy that situation by helping companies use their data to increase the profitability of individual customers, one at a time. Done right, CRM radically transforms customer relationships and expands the business. It helps companies concentrate on the small group of customers who contribute a disproportionately large share of revenues. Successful CRM is about focus, understanding, and the surgical strike.

Unfortunately, most CRM efforts fail. Typical initiatives start in the IT department with high hopes and expensive software but very little in the way of clear business objectives. Once the projects are under way, they are delegated, dissected, and then neglected. It's not surprising that two-thirds of them crash. In many companies, CRM is the fastest-growing segment of IT spending. Yet because of the way most programs have been conceived, they carry as much risk as the enterprise resource planning (ERP) software that proved so disappointing a few years ago.

We believe there is another way to approach CRM. It calls for CEO involvement and senior management direction. It requires an understanding of customer economics, a plan for capturing a greater share of customers' purchases, a focused process from pilot to launch, and a sequence of manageable modules. When it is executed correctly, CRM helps companies establish clear hurdles and checkpoints, as well as generate creative insights to increase the value of the best customers.

An Approach That Works

Successful CRM programs start by gathering such information as

- the net present value of each customer segment
- the cost of serving each segment
- the opportunities for increasing the value of each segment
- the levers available to tap those opportunities

In addition, companies need to develop rigorous metrics for customer acquisition and retention, and for cross-selling opportunities. The objectives are to set goals that the company can achieve and then to extend those wins to other customer segments.

To prove the value of CRM, the first wave of activities should be technically simple yet productive. After companies have established realistic financial projections and goals, they can begin with a modest IT budget to capture the most accessible opportunities. Most important, they should refrain from launching generic programs with indefinite goals, such as "improving our customers' experience."

Once CRM is set in motion, all interactions with customers are touch points for learning more about their unmet needs. The best pattern, we have found, is to build, launch, and improve, and then build, launch, and improve, rather than spend months in preparation before an initial launch. CRM begins with small investments and then leverages financial gains and insights to fuel further product development and marketing.

Finally, senior managers must get onboard early, and line managers and functional heads should be ready to collaborate and share services, as well as manage timelines, checkpoints, and hurdles. As the program continues, each iteration should pay for itself in only 6 to 12 months. Eventually, a company can expect to increase its return on investment at least ten times over. Companies that approach CRM as a process and not an isolated effort understand that they are embarking on a journey of at least five years that will lead to dramatic gains in market share and profitability.

CRM at Work

To appreciate how a well-run CRM program can produce results in a relatively short time, consider the experience of a national sporting-goods retailer we have been working with. The company had been running its three customer channels—catalog, Web site, and store—as separate business units and had not been actively tracking its customers. The senior managers believed they served their "average" customer only once or twice a year. But the team that dug into the customer files found that 20 percent of the customers accounted for 85 percent of the sales volume and more than 100 percent of the profits, considering that some customers are a drain on profits. These best customers ordered more than once a month and bought from six categories of merchandise.

The company's goal for CRM was to develop an integrated, cross-channel view of its customers in order to increase their lifetime value. The first step—establishing a database to see how customers behave in various channels—yielded a number of important insights. The company found that customers who buy through all three channels not only produce the most profits but also spend two to five times more than customers who shop through only one channel. The most profitable customers also have the greatest regard for the brand and can speak with authority about category performance, service quality, and appropriate inventory levels. Our client also found that its best customers were purchasing only half of their category needs from the company.

Armed with these findings, the company issued its first business objectives for CRM:

- Increase customer spending through cross-channel and cross-category programs

- Strengthen marketing programs

- Improve the ease with which customers move across channels

- Focus on understanding the best customers

- Change the game from prospecting for customers to managing relationships with the best ones

Important insights into customer behavior surfaced within a few months, but encouraging customers to change their behavior will take considerably longer. Companies tempted by the 90-day miracles that some CRM programs promise are certain to be disappointed. Our approach will generate significant improvements in only a few months, but large-scale change requires more time.

So far, our client's pilots indicate the likelihood of a greater than 1,000 percent return on investment in the first targeted segment. Over the next three years, the CRM initiative is expected to contribute 8 points to the company's sales-growth rate and deliver a cumulative increase in profitability of more than $300 million.

A Winning Approach to CRM

Our approach to CRM begins with strategy—not technology—and focuses on customer economics and business objectives. It entails the following three steps:

Audit and Strategy Design. Review existing CRM efforts to determine the additional capabilities the company needs, the rate of spending required, and the expected gains.

Program Design. Analyze the economics of customer segments. Assess customers' needs and purchase drivers, and untapped sources of value. Prioritize opportunities; identify appropriate levers, metrics, and milestones; and establish a time frame for results.

Pilot Implementation. Create a plan for launching a pilot or redirecting current initiatives. The pilot should incorporate best-practice learning from past CRM work in such areas as data mining, direct marketing, channel orchestration, sales force automation, and customer service.

To ensure that the above steps are carried out successfully, companies must develop two platforms before launching their programs:

Systems. Despite what many vendors promise, the ability of CRM software to offer end-to-end solutions is still years away. To avoid software quagmires, companies should first establish IT requirements for data storage, analytic systems, and various customer touch points. Instead of "global" CRM efforts, companies should focus on one or two components at a time, such as sales force automation, marketing campaigns, or customer service. This is the only way to make sure that new systems are fully integrated with current ones within a reasonable time.

People. The soft side of CRM must not be underestimated. Before companies start a CRM project, they should bring current organizational structures up to speed, align incentives, and establish a training program for employees who deal directly with customers. Such steps are particularly important for multichannel retailers in companies with many divisions, as well as for companies that offer multipoint services. Unless all service reps and more than half of a company's customer reps use the CRM tools, the program will fail. Finally, organizations must decide what the role of the center will be, how it will enhance cross-divisional cooperation, which parts of the organization will pay the costs, and which ones will get credit for improvements.

*   *   *

The trick in this business is to understand everything there is to know about market segmentation and customer value, and then envision a new way of doing business. As one of our clients put it, "If you don't do that, you're just putting lipstick on a pig."

A successful CRM program is dedicated to the 20 percent of customers who drive 80 percent of the business. Companies shouldn't let horror stories about failed efforts scare them away or delay their decision to start CRM. There's a genuine first-mover advantage in getting the best customers to give you a larger share of their business. CRM is a huge opportunity for a committed company with the right approach—and a huge problem for its competitors.

This article was first published in July 2001.

To Russia with (Cautious) Love

Charbel Ackermann and Stanislav Tsyrlin

Russia seems to be in recovery, but does the country's prognosis justify reinvestment? Earlier this year, The Boston Consulting Group surveyed the leading international players operating in Russia and compared the results with a similar survey carried out in December 1998. Our data indicate that global businesses are once again investing in Russia, although they are proceeding cautiously.

Given the nascent economic recovery and the new government's fiscal and policy reforms, now may be the right time for companies that have shied away from Russia to reassess their position. Without a doubt, Russia—and its consumer markets—have come a long way since the troubles three years ago, but the challenges of doing business there are still considerable. To help consumer goods companies meet those challenges, we have identified some workable strategies.

The Bad Times

In our earlier survey, most international businesses in Russia reported a steep falloff in sales and were expecting further decreases. The survey came in the wake of a collapsing economy and a decimated ruble; the consensus was that it would take three full years for consumer-goods and pharmaceutical sales to climb back to just 80 percent of their 1997 levels. Nonetheless, most of the global consumer-goods companies that had built businesses in Russia decided to tough it out, even if that meant substantial losses.

To make it through the hard times, they downscaled their operations, adapted product ranges to budget-conscious consumers, and converted costs—where possible—into devalued rubles. Two-thirds of the companies we surveyed reduced their work force, and nearly half cut compensation for their remaining personnel. Distribution all but stopped, and companies struggled to find the right balance between national and regional coverage. Few of them committed new money to the market, but most ongoing investments, especially in local production, were completed.

Coming Back

Our latest survey, which captures the effects of the rebound that began last year, indicates a greatly improved outlook. Most players anticipate consistent growth and see no sign of a return to the erratic macroeconomic policies of the past. Political stability is noticeably stronger, and the government is making regulatory improvements, albeit slowly. Consumer goods companies are maintaining streamlined yet differentiated product ranges and are expanding distribution to compete with increasingly aggressive local players.

Most of the companies in our survey experienced sales growth of 25 to 60 percent in Russia during 2000. Moreover, whereas only one-third of the companies had been profitable in 1999, more than half were in 2000, and fewer than 15 percent reported a loss. To be sure, the dollar revenues of consumer goods companies were still hovering between just 50 and 65 percent of 1997 levels. But that shouldn't be the case for long. In fact, during the first half of 2001, most companies increased their sales by 25 to 40 percent and were forecasting annual compound growth rates (in U.S. dollars) above 15 percent for fast-moving consumer goods and around 10 percent for consumer durables and pharmaceuticals.

Russia Today

Our data indicate that Russia is coming around again as international players begin to make plans for increasing opportunities there. Here are some snapshots of the current environment:

Consumer Markets. After the crisis of 1998, local producers gained volume market share because consumers grew more price sensitive. Shoppers are still concerned about price, but their interest in value is on the rise. Consequently, local producers that compete only on price are losing out to those that offer both low price and high quality. In fact, some improved local products are beginning to compete against foreign brands. Foreign brands that didn't have fixed assets in Russia at the time of the crisis weakened their position by closing rep offices and instead selling through distributors. Many of them are now trying to reenter at the high end of the market. As for consumers, regional differences remain significant: many shoppers are used to thinking in terms of rubles, not dollars, and some are nostalgic for traditional Russian products.

Pricing. Except for a few high-end products, most international companies have reduced prices in response to the crisis. They also continue to market products with local appeal, although many companies are beginning to introduce new products from their global portfolios. In addition, more than half of the companies surveyed have repositioned existing products toward the low end, and almost one-third are introducing or adapting traditional Russian brands.

Distribution. More than two-thirds of the companies we surveyed have shifted their focus to alternative distribution channels and have added new channels, such as the restaurant and catering channels for food producers. Although credit management remains an issue, more than half of the companies have introduced more relaxed terms and payment plans.

Sales Force. Most foreign companies have begun to expand their operations again, although gradually. Nearly half have added employees, and as many as 30 percent doubled their staff during 2000.

Local Investment. International companies are showing a renewed interest in Russian investments. Two-thirds of the surveyed companies are reinvesting in local production, half are spending more on brand building, and just under half are investing in supply-base improvements.

Economic Prospects. In 1997 the purchasing power of the dollar was 1.4 times higher in Russia than in the United States. After devaluation, it was 3 times higher. We predict that the real value of the ruble will be more than 80 percent of its 1997 level by 2006, at which point Russia's GDP will reach its 1997 value of $440 billion. That amounts to 4 percent real annual growth during the next five years. By 2006, the purchasing power of the dollar in Russia will be at a level comparable to that in the other economies of Central and Eastern Europe.

Risks to Consider

We expect that most consumer markets in Russia will enjoy double-digit growth (in U.S. dollars) over the next few years. The question is whether that growth will be sustainable if the price of oil goes down to its forecasted median of $21 per barrel. Other risks include appreciation of the ruble fueled by uncontrolled inflation, lack of follow-through on tax and customs regulations, and only modest progress on industrial restructuring and other reforms.

Risks seem moderate on the political front. The government is focusing on centralizing power but is leaving fundamental social issues alone. As a result, general political stability can be expected. The government's tough position on Chechnya and tighter controls on tax flows have led the main proponents of independence from Moscow—Tatarstan and Bashkortostan, for example—to temper their aggressive postures. Indeed, political apathy is high: even deprived of basic services, people in the far eastern regions have not engaged in organized protest. However, if the government continues not to provide such services, one can expect a crisis. The signs would be visible well in advance, though, and for now we do not see any.

Meeting Russia's Challenges

Russia's mixed prognosis notwithstanding, we believe that expectations of consistent economic growth, manageable inflation, increasing real incomes, rising urban employment, and income tax reform provide sufficient reason for consumer goods companies to consider cautious investments in local manufacturing, brand building, and new distribution relationships. Here are the major challenges that consumer goods companies will face in Russia and some strategies for meeting them:

Sales. Volumes are at precrisis levels but still below where they were expected to be at this point. To attract new customers, companies must create more occasions for impulse purchases and educate household decision makers about the value of their products.

Customers. Russian consumers are increasingly interested in value, but many are still sensitive to price. To attract both segments, companies can offer high-quality, reasonably priced products while maintaining inexpensive brands. In addition, if consumers prefer traditional products, companies should develop a deeper understanding of those consumers' needs and introduce local brands.

Pricing. The prices of foreign brands with low value added will continue to be linked to the dollar, at least in the short term, while the prices of local brands will be based on the ruble. For high-end brands, prices should reflect value but remain competitive against important local players. For low-end brands, companies should follow the market price if margins allow. Local manufacturing can help reduce costs.

Branding. Because consumers are switching to more expensive products, maintaining brand awareness will be crucial. Television advertising is the most cost-effective channel in Russia. Commercials should focus on a product's superior value-price ratio.

Distribution. Russia's distribution system remains fragmented, but direct delivery and new channels are becoming increasingly important. Companies should consider adding local distribution and sales capabilities as well as local production. Offering credit, flexible payment conditions, and consignment options will help companies maintain good relationships with regional distributors. Finally, companies can seek direct delivery through distributors or their own sales force, and establish relationships with new channels.

*   *   *

Rumors of Russia's demise have been premature. The country has had several years of pain and suffering, but it is on the mend. With stable rates of inflation, increasing real incomes, higher employment, and tax reform, Russia once again looks like a promising opportunity.

This article was first published in August 2001.

Workonomics: Helping Retailers Value Human Capital

Rainer Strack, Alexander Lintner, and Matthias Bolz

In 1977 a *Forbes* journalist accompanied the founder and CEO of a remarkably successful U.S. retail chain through a typical day. The writer's ensuing article described a grueling schedule of visits to one store after another and conversations with hundreds of employees. Listening to their problems, praising their performance, and offering his advice, the CEO was developing a companywide sense of cohesion that would become legendary. The journalist wrote that the company leader tended his people "like plants in a garden, nourishing with praise, advancement, and good pay, transplanting constantly to improve the mix, weeding where necessary." The article's subject was, of course, Sam Walton, chairman and CEO of Wal-Mart Stores.

Walton was ahead of his time in viewing his employees not as *cost centers* that ought to be rationalized but as assets who should be cultivated and managed. That's hardly a revolutionary insight today. To compete in the current marketplace, senior executives know they must attract and retain the best people. Their efforts to do so, however, expose a serious limitation in many companies: their management systems for measuring performance are geared to the efficient use of capital, not people. In practice, company assessments rarely consider *human* capital.

To be sure, optimizing fixed and working capital is critical for improving financial returns in capital-intensive businesses. Conventional reporting systems and measurements—such as return on investment (ROI), which assesses the productivity of capital investments—were developed for that purpose. But those systems and measures are less useful in retail businesses, where investments in human resources are typically high. In fact, The Boston Consulting Group has found that in Europe's largest retail chains, personnel costs are often three to four times higher than capital costs. (See Exhibit 1.)

A New Approach

To help executives make the most of their assets in people-intensive industries, BCG has developed an approach called Workonomics. We have designed Workonomics to answer the same questions about employees' performance that conventional measurement-and-control systems answer about capital performance. This approach provides quantitative, personnel-oriented metrics that mirror classic control systems and bridge the gap between measures of capital and assessment of human assets.

Workonomics links traditional measures of employees' productivity (for example, sales per employee, employee hours per store, and employee turnover) with the financial performance of each store and region, and with various corporate functions. To complement ROI in people-intensive indus-

Exhibit 1

Human Capital Can Outweigh Investment Capital

European retailers	Residual income per person	Value added per person	Average cost per person	Ratio of personnel costs to capital costs
		(in thousands of euros)		
Sainsbury	5	33	28	3:1
Tesco	5	26	21	2:1
Safeway (U.K.)	4	27	23	2:1
Laurus	3	24	21	4:1
Asda Group	3	27	24	2:1
Carrefour	2	27	25	2:1
Royal Ahold	2	24	22	3:1
Delhaize Group	2	21	19	4:1
Douglas Group	2	34	32	4:1
Hornbach Holding	1	33	32	2:1
AVA	1	32	31	7:1
Groupe Casino	0	20	20	2:1
Karstadt Quelle	−1	34	35	4:1
SinnLeffers	−2	34	36	3:1

SOURCE: BCG analysis.
NOTE: Capital costs equal the sum of weighted average cost of capital times invested capital plus depreciation.

tries, for instance, Workonomics calculates value added per person (VAP) as a measure of average productivity. Subtracting the average cost per person (ACP) from VAP and multiplying the difference by the number of employed people (P) produces the residual income, which is called either economic value added (EVA) or cash value added (CVA). (For fuller definitions, see the glossary at the end of this article.)

An increase in EVA or CVA means higher shareholder value. Thus, employee productivity, or VAP, is directly connected to either EVA or CVA, the core financial metric that is used in many companies. The purpose of Workonomics is not to replace old, capital-based control systems; rather, it is to make them more realistic by incorporating a measure of human capital and linking that measure directly to shareholder value.

Workonomics also lets a retailer continuously monitor the effectiveness of its current operating model for various regions, formats, and functions. Using the VAP calculations for comparable stores, managers can identify high and low levels of productivity and determine the potential for increasing value.

Drilling Down to Individual Stores

Companies can apply Workonomics at all levels of their operations. For example, on the level of the branch store, a company might break down Workonomics metrics to single out such value levers as the fluctuation rate (employee turnover) or the sickness ratio. The company could then conduct a sensitivity analysis to determine which of those performance levers are most likely to affect EVA or CVA if they change. Thus, Workonomics identifies the levers that are most directly related to shareholder value and provides a significant advantage over the traditional balanced-scorecard approach.

Furthermore, a branch store's value levers can be visually represented in a computer program. (See Exhibit 2.) The "Workonomics Cockpit" shows how one store can be measured against all the other stores in a company's chain. Each horizontal bar, or lever, compares the store's performance in a specific category against the performance of other stores and rates it from worst, on the left, to best, on the right. The darker shading indicates a need for action, and the lighter shading signals above-average value. The wider the shaded area—light or dark—the greater the distance from average. Therefore, a wide lightly shaded area is very good and a wide dark area very

Exhibit 2

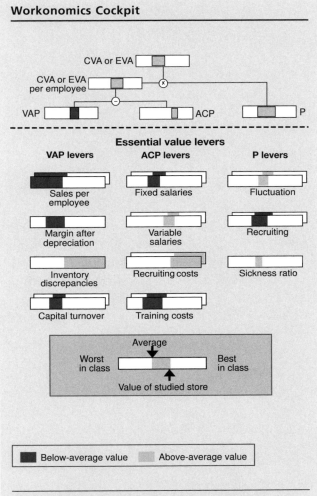

Workonomics Cockpit

SOURCE: The Boston Consulting Group.
NOTE: CVA = cash value added; EVA = economic value added; VAP = value added per person; ACP = average cost per person; P = number of employed people.

bad. The average falls at different points within the levers, depending on the value being measured.

The levers in the upper section of the exhibit show the key financial metric—CVA or EVA—as a product of the new, personnel-oriented metrics described above: VAP, ACP, and P. The "essential value levers" in the lower part of the exhibit are all of the component measures for assessing VAP, ACP, and P. By double-clicking on most of those value levers, managers can drill down to more detailed metrics. (A doubled image denotes that feature.)

Under the "fluctuation" lever, for example, attrition in the work force might be quantified along three dimensions: whether the company wanted the employee to leave; the employee's position in the company's hierarchy (for example, branch store head, department head, or sales staff); and subsequent employment (did the employee move to another industry, go to a competitor, or transfer within the company?). Not only would the fluctuation measure provide early warning of problems with the sales staff at individual stores—the telltale sign would be an increase in defections to competitors—it would also measure the direct quantitative effect of the rate of turnover on critical financial ratios.

To get a picture of back-office efficiency at a branch store, managers can double-click the "sales per employee" lever to reveal sales per sales employee and the number of sales employees compared with the number of total employees at the branch store. Going even deeper, managers can also target the sales per sales employee of a department or product group.

Thus, Workonomics establishes an analytic link between productivity and the key financial ratio. If managers use these benchmarks to compare stores with similar competitive positions, locations, and purchasing practices, they will gain a very clear picture of the average employee's current productivity and the potential for improvement in each store, department, or product group.

In effect, Workonomics shines a spotlight on those areas that require immediate action, and it gives the personnel department a strategic tool to use alongside the capital-based control measures of the finance department. Such close, rigorous tracking helps managers make better decisions for each store—for example, whether to add incentives or tighten costs; whether to invest in more service or reduce employees' hours; and whether to change employees' profiles or invest in their development.

Workonomics assessments of what employees contribute and how the productivity of one group compares with that of others are every bit as accurate as comparisons of capital performance. Moreover, as a Workonomics analysis of the recent success of one U.K. chain, Tesco, demonstrates, increases in shareholder value can be traced directly to increases in productivity.

Tesco's Revival

In the mid-1980s, retailers had such a poor image, especially among graduates of secondary school, that it was difficult for Tesco to recruit the right people. Concerned about its long-term prospects, Tesco devised a centralized program for recruiting graduates of secondary school and college. At the same time, to make middle and upper management more productive, the company redefined jobs and responsibilities. As a result, Tesco reduced the number of management levels from six to three and eliminated 4,000 managerial positions. Highly productive employees were brought onboard, and unproductive ones were let go. The employees who survived the cut were granted more flexibility, and motivation improved.

Using Workonomics to assess Tesco's success, we determined that VAP increased 60 percent over the last ten years as a result of the company's efforts in human resources. In fact, of all the retail companies we analyzed, Tesco achieved the second-highest residual income per employee. (See Exhibit 1.) It's not surprising that Tesco is now considered one of the world's premier operators of supermarkets and hypermarkets. Thanks to its decision to nurture its people as valuable assets, Tesco employs the right number of people, they have the right skills, they are in the right places, and they are doing the right jobs. For the roughly 100 positions it advertises each year, the company now receives some 5,000 applications from graduates of the best colleges and universities.

*   *   *

As Sam Walton told the *Forbes* journalist, "We like to let folks know we're interested in them and that they're vital to us. 'Cause they are." But it's not just interest that is urgently needed. To manage in a way that employees as well as shareholders perceive as fair, logical, and financially sound, retailers must have a rigorously quantitative system for monitoring and managing their operations. Workonomics provides that system.

Retailers need to know whether their employees are as productive as their competitors' employees. How much value do their employees create? Exactly where are their problems and what should they do about them? To questions such as these that have long concerned only finance departments, Workonomics is the first system that delivers quantitative answers.

Workonomics belongs to a set of new value-management concepts that BCG calls The Real Asset Value Enhancer. RAVE merges value management and balanced scorecards into Balanced Value Management. Aside from Workonomics, the most advanced RAVE concept is Custonomics, which measures the productivity of investments in customers. For further information about Workonomics, please visit our Web site at www.workonomics.bcg.com.

This article was first published in September 2001.

A Workonomics Glossary

Value-Based Measures: The Capital View
Because these metrics refer to invested capital, we call this the capital view.

Economic value added (EVA) measures earnings that exceed the cost of capital. EVA is calculated by subtracting the weighted average cost of capital from the return on investment (ROI) and multiplying the difference by the amount of invested capital.

Cash value added (CVA) is the equivalent of EVA on the cash flow side. EVA is defined by yields, and CVA is defined by cash flow. Here ROI is analogous to cash flow return on investment (CFROI). EVA and CVA are also sometimes called residual income.

Workonomics Measures: The Human Resources View
Value added per person (VAP) measures the average productivity of employees. To obtain this measure, subtract all costs—including the cost of capital but excluding personnel costs—from sales. Then divide the difference by the number of employed people (P). VAP is analogous to ROI or CFROI in the capital view.

Average cost per person (ACP) denotes the average personnel cost per employee. ACP corresponds to the cost of capital in the capital view.

Number of employed people (P) denotes the full-time equivalents employed by a company, branch store, or other entity. P corresponds to invested capital in the capital view.

In the human resources view, EVA and CVA are calculated by subtracting ACP from VAP and multiplying the difference by P. In this way, the company's key ratio—either EVA or CVA—is broken down into three personnel-oriented metrics.

Finding New Value in Legacy Assets

Michael S. Deimler, George Stalk Jr., and Jim Whitehurst

Great companies make good things happen even in bad times. Now, squeezed by the constraints of a sluggish economy, the greatest consumer companies are once again earning their stripes by creating new value from legacy assets. In some cases, these companies have learned how to exploit old assets in novel ways, occasionally enlisting the Internet in the effort. In other cases, they are finding value in assets that no one ever considered valuable before. In both situations, the result is additional sources of growth and profitability for core businesses.

To take advantage of such opportunities, companies need to adopt a far more expansive view of what constitutes an asset and how best to realize value from it. They must also develop the capabilities and processes for systematically redeploying their assets to create new businesses.

The Hard Value of Soft Assets

According to the traditional view, an asset is anything that appears on the balance sheet—for example, fixed assets such as property, plant, and equipment, or current assets such as inventory and cash. In the new economy, this view is unnecessarily limiting. Some of a company's most important assets are so-called soft assets, which don't show up on the balance sheet—for example, customer information, intellectual property, and management reputation. Most companies are vaguely aware of the potential worth embedded in such assets. But few go to the trouble of creating a comprehensive inventory of their soft assets with explicit plans for realizing that potential.

The exhibit "Creating a Complete Inventory of Assets" illustrates how such an inventory might be developed—starting with the traditional balance-sheet items and then moving to less obvious assets, such as supplier relationships, loyalty programs, and employees' attributes. When organizations take a broader view of what constitutes an asset, they are often surprised by just how many opportunities they have.

One company that is well aware of its opportunities is Starbucks, an organization that has been particularly innovative in leveraging a wide range of traditional and not-so-traditional assets. Among its most obvious assets is, of course, its well-known brand, which draws customers into its outlets as well as to products such as Frappuccino, the popular coffee drink. If the brand brings customers into a Starbucks store, it can also attract them to other businesses, such as bookstores and airlines. That drawing power has caught the attention of Barnes & Noble and United Air Lines, which have formed partnerships with Starbucks that allow them to sell its coffee. They benefit by offering customers a desirable product, and Starbucks gains additional distribution points.

In addition to its brand, Starbucks has at least two other valuable, albeit less obvious, assets. One is its loyal (some might say addicted) customer base of high-earning, highly educated consumers. Another is a retail presence across the United States and other parts of the world that is around 3,000 stores strong and growing. Starbucks looked at how those assets might be leveraged and came up with some innovative ideas to enrich its brand, attract more customers, and generate revenue.

One project is a partnership with Microsoft to introduce wireless Internet access over the next two years in nearly three-quarters of Starbucks stores. Since most customers tend to settle in after buying their coffee—reading, chatting, or working on their laptops—offering wireless service seems a natural next step. Through this partnership, Microsoft hopes to increase usage of its MSN portal and build loyalty with a very attractive, Internet-savvy consumer segment. For its part, Starbucks is looking to sell more coffee, both to established patrons who stop by more frequently to check their e-mail and to new customers drawn in by the service.

Capturing the Value

Once a company has created a comprehensive inventory of the various types of hard and soft assets it can exploit, it must figure out precisely how to realize value from them.

Creating a Complete Inventory of Assets

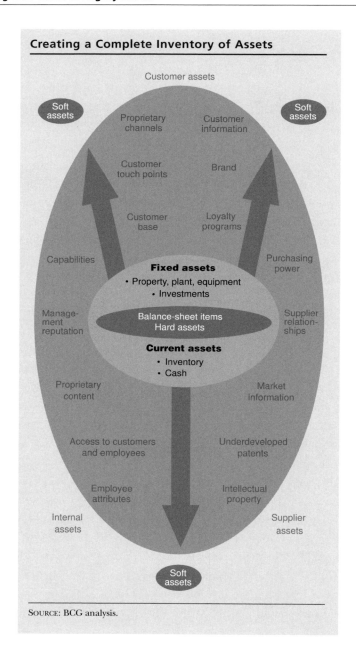

SOURCE: BCG analysis.

In some cases, legacy assets can quickly be monetized—as DuPont has discovered. Each year the company spends billions of dollars to research and register around 350 patents, many of which don't yield any returns. So DuPont decided to triage its patent portfolio according to each patent's intrinsic value, its value to the company, and its value to others. Patents that are no longer valuable to anyone, as well as those with a short shelf life, are allowed to expire.

There is, however, another group of patents that are no longer worthwhile to the company but are still worth something to others. DuPont has come up with a couple of creative ways to leverage those sleeping assets. One venture is a Web site called yet2.com, which DuPont formed with a consortium of 11 other companies for the purpose of selling patents. But that still leaves the patents for technologies that might be valuable someday but aren't yet ripe for licensing. The solution: give them away. DuPont has made such gifts to three universities, reaping a tax write-off of $64 million.

Other companies have discovered how to leverage the value of human assets. Porsche, for example, employs some 2,000 of the world's best auto engineers even though it manufactures only a few models. The company views itself not just as a producer of luxury cars but also as a supplier of engineering genius. It didn't take a great intuitive leap for Porsche to realize that it could outsource its R&D capability to other automakers, such as Volkswagen. That move has brought in as much as $30 million per year in incremental revenue.

Beyond generating income, a company's existing assets can often provide the kernel for the creation of platform businesses that the company sets up on its own or with partners. The most important of these ventures target fundamental improvements in the economics of the core business. For instance, Delta Air Lines has established an online portal for small-business travelers called Mind Your Own Business Travel (MYOBTravel.com). The venture uses the Internet to serve a segment of travelers that was prohibitively expensive to reach in the past. Other platform businesses allow a company to deepen its bonds with existing customers and create new sources of revenue. For example, Delta is forming partnerships with wireless companies to start a number of businesses that will give travelers uninterrupted wireless access on the ground and in the air.

An "Out-of-Body" Experience

Exploiting hidden assets is an "out-of-body" experience for most companies. An industry-specific mindset can make it hard for managers to recognize alternative uses for their assets. Traditional planning processes don't encourage the kind of fresh thinking necessary to identify new opportunities, and funding processes are slow and inflexible. New capabilities are required for success.

The first essential capability is a clear strategic focus. The evolution of new-economy businesses remains highly uncertain. Still, no company can afford to wait until the future becomes clear, for the simple reason that the choices players make now will shape their industries. A company needs to establish a sense of direction that is flexible enough to let the organization adapt to unanticipated changes. Managers and employees must be able to filter the many opportunities that come their way and identify the ones that are truly important.

Another capability a company needs is a supercharged business-development group. Such groups are staffed with savvy dealmakers who know how to form nontraditional partnerships and alliances rapidly, and can recognize when a particular opportunity fits—or clashes with—a company's core strategy. To that end, Delta has established a full-time ventures group that reports to the CFO and identifies and vets potential strategic partners and deals.

A third key area of expertise is new-business creation. A company must be able to mobilize teams quickly to "road test" new business models and launch the most promising ones. At many companies, incubation teams help accelerate the development of new platform businesses.

*   *   *

Extracting new value from legacy assets represents the next wave of value creation at large, established consumer companies. But to do it right, senior managers must oversee the wholesale transformation of the way their companies conceive of assets. They will need to help their companies identify new opportunities for creating value from those assets and then act to exploit them—whether by creating new businesses or restructuring the old.

This article was first published in October 2001.

Paying for Performance:
An Overlooked Opportunity

Paul Gordon

Every time a sales representative considers which customers to pursue, how aggressively, with what mix of products and services, and at what prices, he or she is implementing the company's strategy—or working against it. Sales force deployment and compensation are, therefore, among the most strategic levers a company has to improve growth, market share, and profitability. If sales reps' compensation is not aligned with the company's strategy, the strategy will not be implemented.

A client of The Boston Consulting Group points out that "good sales reps will quickly strip apart a comp plan and figure out where to devote their time for maximum payout. They might not understand our strategy. They might not know very much about the product. They might not be willing to invest time to learn about the customer. But they seem to know intuitively what will put money in their pockets."

Few companies have payout schemes that are aligned with company growth and profitability. (See Exhibit 1.) In some companies, the compensation plan was not kept current with changing drivers of success. In other companies, the plan's original designers didn't fully understand the profitability and growth potential of all their products and customer segments. Yet most consumer companies could greatly improve sales and margins in less than six months if they would take the time to link their compensation systems with their strategy.

An effective compensation plan aligns sales force rewards with the company's goals, measures performance precisely and fairly, encourages sales-

Exhibit 1

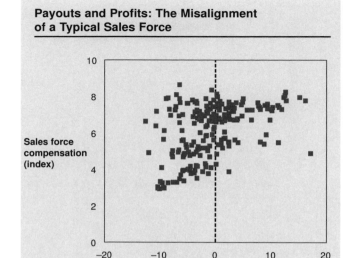

Payouts and Profits: The Misalignment of a Typical Sales Force

SOURCE: BCG analysis.

people to stretch their efforts, and provides rewards that attract and retain the best performers. A poorly designed plan, by contrast, can unwittingly direct the sales force to focus on the wrong customers, encourage unnecessary discounting, and overpay for poor performance. It can also inhibit teamwork and discourage the sales force from taking the time to educate customers about new products.

The Price of a Misaligned Compensation Plan

Consider the case of a manufacturer whose revenues, market share, and margins were all declining, even though the company still owned the greatest share of a concentrated market and its customers faced substantial switching costs in shifting to another vendor. The company had been unable to introduce profitable new upgrades to its existing customers, and it had been losing accounts to its competitors. Most of its problems, it turned out, could be traced to its compensation plan.

For example, sales rewards were based only on revenues (not profits) from sales of new systems and upgrades. The profit margin on upgrades, after selling costs, was much higher than for new systems. But because revenues from upgrades were only one-fifth of revenues from new systems and upgrades required more sales effort per dollar of revenue, the sales force pushed new systems rather than upgrades. Furthermore, because the salespeople were not compensated for service contracts, they focused their energies on selling large new systems. In many cases, that meant going after competitors' accounts rather than mining the company's customer base.

Selling new systems was difficult, however. And because it often involved winning over competitors' customers, who would face high switching costs, the company provided extra incentives for "customer conversions." (In one instance, a new Mercedes was awarded to the salesperson who converted the most customers of a specific competitor.) Moreover, the company had given the sales force substantial authority to determine prices. The cumulative effect of these features of the compensation system was to undermine the whole company. The sales force focused on competitors' accounts, ignored product upgrades in favor of high-ticket items, used price as a lever to overcome the switching barriers, and even started a price war. And because much of the sales force was ignoring the existing customer base, market share was falling.

Getting the Basics Right

A good incentive plan should answer three basic questions: Who is paid? How much are they paid? What level of performance are they paid for? Furthermore, the plan should reflect the company's strategy and the value it offers its customers. And it should be precise, fair, and simple.

By aligning incentives with strategy, the company ensures that the sales force focuses on the most attractive customers, selling them the right product mix at the right price. Precision is important because it guarantees that salespeople are rewarded only for those aspects of the selling process over which they have control. A fair plan means that equal stretch gets equal reward. And a plan that is simple, having no more than four or five components, will be easy to communicate to others. Precision, fairness, and simplicity are critical qualities because good salespeople tend also to be skilled cryptographers. They quickly decode any new compensation plan and figure out how to get the most out of it. When they do that with a precise, fair, and simple plan, however, they are also figuring out how the company will get the most out of the plan as well.

Design Logic

Understanding the basic goals of a compensation plan is challenge enough, but designing a program that carries them out can be a truly difficult task. All compensation systems involve a series of complex tradeoffs. How much of the compensation should be fixed and how much variable? Should it reward revenues, profit margins, or both? How will it weigh mature products against new ones? How will it encourage salespeople to stretch for incremental dollars once they have hit their quotas? The right answers to these questions will balance the salesperson's primary concern ("Is my return worth the effort I put out?") with the company's performance, its strategic and financial goals, and the value it offers its customers. Here's how this tradeoff might be managed in three important compensation issues:

Balancing Volume and Margins. Many companies wrestle with whether to base compensation on revenues or profits (usually total gross-margin dollars). If salespeople are compensated for revenue only, they have a tendency to trade price for volume and to spend less time selling lower-ticket (but often more profitable) items. If they are compensated for gross-margin dollars, they are tempted to cut price on high-margin products in order to sell more of them (even if the market will bear the higher price), and they neglect low-margin products.

As a result, they forgo opportunities that might be less profitable to them personally but more profitable to the company overall. To avoid such practices, the company can create a payout matrix that rewards both revenue and margin targets. Although the matrix adds a little complexity, the sales force will have no trouble decoding it, and it offers an elegant way of achieving the volume-margin balance.

Managing the Product Portfolio. In most companies, salespeople have a bundle of products to sell. These products are at various points in their life cycle, so they have different levels of strategic importance and requirements for positioning; and selling them involves varying amounts of time for customer education. Unless the compensation plan reflects the strategy for each product, a salesperson might simply favor his or her own interest. That can have a huge impact on sales of products that are in the early years of their life cycle, when the sales effort per dollar of revenue can be high, as well as for products at the end of their cycle, when they require an extra push to keep sales moving. A good plan considers the return to the salesperson for each incremental hour of effort and adjusts the reward associated with each product to reflect the company's strategic objectives, the product's financial characteristics, and the customer's value proposition.

In a recent project, BCG's team asked salespeople to estimate the incremental rate they required for an incremental hour of work. Annual cash compensation for each rep working 46 hours per week averaged $47,000. The salespeople determined that for an additional $1,000 per year, they would devote an additional hour every week to new-product sales. The company was then able to set up a temporary incentive program aimed at increasing the time its sales force gave to its new product line.

Ensuring Stretch Performance. Many companies have compensation plans that pay out a portion of a bonus whenever a salesperson achieves a predetermined portion of his or her quota. For example, 50 percent of a quota earns 50 percent of a bonus, 75 percent earns 75 percent, and so forth until the full quota is reached. Exhibit 2 illustrates the difference between that approach and one that makes no payout until 80 percent of a quota is achieved. At that point, it increases the incremental return for sales beyond the quota. The problem with the former approach is that it inadvertently rewards underperformers—people who, for example, achieve only half of their quotas—and it encourages the stars to coast once they have reached their goals. A reward line with a steeper slope motivates sales reps to stretch to achieve the first 80 percent quickly and to keep stretching for additional rewards once they surpass their quotas.

Design Process

Designing a compensation system is an iterative process that requires continuous testing and refining to ensure that the incremental return for each unit of sales effort is consistent with the company's goals. The first step is to gather clear data on the following:

- Product and customer profitability, after-selling costs, and adjustments for win rate

- Strategic objectives for each product

- The average sales effort required for each product

- Variability of sales performance and drivers of that performance

- Number of potential sales and length of the sales cycle (If a salesperson makes only two or three big sales a year, the company should introduce some form of multiyear averaging.)

Exhibit 2   **An Aggressive Compensation System**
Can Stretch Performance

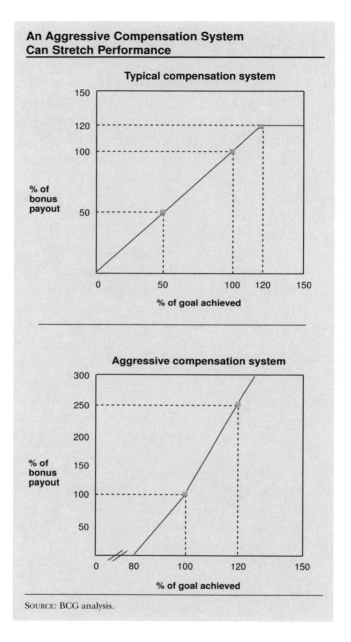

SOURCE: BCG analysis.

Once the historical data are solid, the company can develop a number of plans for optimizing the incremental dollars per hour of sales effort. To understand how these plans might influence sales behavior, the company should test the plans with focus groups of salespeople. With the results of this research, the company can refine the plan that is most likely to achieve the desired results, develop communication and support tools, and roll out the program.

Indeed, this is the process the manufacturing company followed when it discovered that it could resolve most of its problems by revising its compensation system. The result was a plan that took into account all revenue sources—not just sales of new systems and upgrades—and awarded points on the basis of a combination of revenues and profit margins. The company also addressed the requirements of products at various stages of their life cycle by applying multiplier factors to products that needed an extra sales push. And finally, it established a steeper reward-for-achievement slope. Working together, these revisions greatly improved the company's performance. The company stopped losing market share, pricing became more rational, and revenues per customer increased because the sales force was selling a greater range of products to existing customers.

* * *

If it has been some time since you last looked closely at your compensation system, chances are it no longer supports your strategy for providing value to your customers and achieving superior returns. Here are ten warning signs that could indicate that your compensation system needs an overhaul:

- Your highest-paid salespeople are not the ones who are generating the most profitability for the company

- You are losing share with your most attractive customers

- Price realization for similar types of customers varies widely

- You are having a hard time getting the sales force to sell the full range of your products

- Product introductions falter for lack of attention from the sales force

- You are paying more than 90 percent of the sales force some kind of bonus

- Salespeople stop selling as soon as they achieve their quotas

- To determine payout levels, you first need to process a lot of exceptions

- Customer complaints are rising, and they point to problems with the sales force

- No salesperson can make more than you do

Nearly every consumer-goods company doing business today could quickly and dramatically improve its bottom line by rethinking its sales force's compensation in light of its strategy, financial objectives, and the value it offers its customers. If you have doubts about alignment and congruence, invite your best and worst reps to lunch and ask them these questions:

- What are our least profitable and most profitable businesses, and how do they affect our selling efforts?

- What products are we pushing, and why are we pushing them?

- When you make more money, does the company make more money?

This article was first published in November 2001.

Wanted: Leaders and Diagnosticians

Michael Silverstein, Jeff Gell, and Kent Owens

It is hard to imagine a more difficult year—and a more trying business environment—than the one we've just come through. Terror. Market instability. Consumer fear. Rising world unemployment. Government spending without visible short-term results.

Now is a time for courage and rejuvenation. We need strong leaders and a redoubled resolution for investment, growth, and improved performance. It is time to take a lesson or two from the past. In the final installment of this year's Opportunities for Action series, we want to turn again to history for perspective.

Great nations are born out of a sense of heroic invention. Similarly, each of our companies at birth carried with it a sense of invention. We came to work without preconceived notions. Every day was exciting. Every week offered new opportunities. Our recruiting was radical, often bringing in people with unusual skill and energy. The environment was chaotic, filled with trial by fire and the surprise of success. The effective leader provided vision, tenacity, and instinct, and made wise preemptive investments.

Unfortunately, companies often lose the characteristics that originally propelled them ahead. Professional managers replace the visionary founders, introducing formal processes and controls. Leaders lose the passion of their youth. They assume defensive positions to protect their legacy, and in so doing provide opportunities for rivals to breach their markets.

Established companies often see themselves as mature. They ignore or minimize outsider innovation. They live by outdated and irreconcilable rules of thumb, and often their leadership appears awkward and indecisive. The leaders' market antennae are often atrophied or destroyed.

Rejuvenators take mature companies to a new level. They make radical decisions. They ignore legacy rules and redefine a better future. They seek outside ideas and make them a source of organizational oxygen.

Rome as an Analogy for Business: The Rise and Fall

The epic rise and fall of ancient Rome serves as a cautionary tale about creative spark dissipated by carelessness, arrogance, and inattention. If we could go back to the Roman Empire in 218 B.C., we would find the world to be a fearful place. Warring tribes use primitive and brutal means to plunder and enslave their enemies. People eat only what they can harvest, facing starvation in bad years on a diet of bread, water, and a trace of wine. It is a lawless world. Thomas Hobbes, the political historian, artfully captured it: "The life of man: solitary, poor, nasty, brutish, and short."

In 202 B.C., the Romans repelled Hannibal and drove his elephant cavalry from the Italian peninsula. The victory over Hannibal removed Carthage as a threat. (See Exhibit 1.) What was Rome at that point? A loose alliance with a handful of principles that would ultimately carry it to world domination.

The Romans had a sense of unity and an imperative to create wealth and power, which held them together as a conquering people. The early Romans believed that they could conquer the Mediterranean region. Achieving

Exhibit 1   **The Birth of an Empire**

The Republic of Rome After Hannibal Was Repelled in 202 B.C.

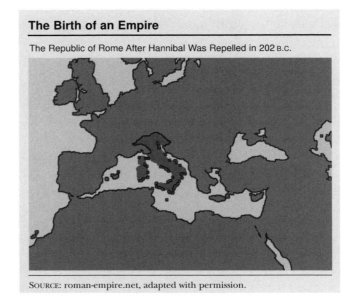

SOURCE: roman-empire.net, adapted with permission.

improvements in productivity to create a surplus, they then used that surplus to provide Roman citizens with access to wealth and monuments of success. Ambition and organization were the foundations of that success.

For five centuries, the Romans lived by four principles: domain expertise, continuous invention, succession planning, and process engineering to deliver productivity advantage. These principles can form the basis of greater success for your company, too.

Domain Expertise. The Romans initially employed domain expertise in their military service. Although average life expectancy at the time was only 32 years, soldiers signed up in their teens for a full 20 years of service. That was considered the minimum amount of time to become a master archer, catapult operator, swordsman, or battlefield commander.

When they invaded north into what is now France and Germany, the Romans introduced precision, experience, training, discipline, technology, and expertise. At its peak, the Roman army was fixed at 28 legions, with a full legion consisting of approximately 5,000 men. The legions were based in the conquered territories and spread the "culture" of Rome. Each legion brought, on average, 50,000 man-years of experience and expertise to each engagement. No army in the world could beat the Romans on the battlefield. At the end of the 20-year term, surviving soldiers received a generous pension: land, money, and honors. Compare that 20-year term and depth of experience to the average time people spend in their jobs at your company.

Continuous Invention. The Romans defined this as product development engineering and application for technological advantage. Roman engineering was a marvel in its time. No one before had so fully understood the power of infrastructure in the form of water supply and road construction. A safe water supply was the critical ingredient for building cities. Cities resulted in specialization and productivity increases. Productivity provided the surplus that gave Rome its ability to rule. Roads permitted quick deployment of troops for command and control.

The public monuments engineered by the Romans still stand throughout Europe and the Middle East. No competitor could match the Romans for speed in building bridges and siege-works. Behind the Roman army were the world's first mass manufacturers—producers of helmets, armor, and weapons.

Roman technical skill was applied not only to large-scale construction projects—roads, aqueducts, and mines—but also to the manufacture of pottery, glassware, and other goods. The Romans created the first global consumer-goods supply chain: grain from Egypt, seafood from the southern Mediterranean, wine from France, and silk from the Middle East all made it regularly to the capital of the empire. The military-industrial complex's need for innovations pulled technology forward. Profits were counted in the form of conquered territory and new tax revenue.

The Romans built according to a formula. Their hold on the provinces was secured by forts placed at every major point of control. Every fort in the empire had five major buildings: a grain storage facility, a bathhouse, a hospital, the commander's house, and a barracks for the troops. That design allowed for scale, efficiency, and an experience curve benefit. (See Exhibits 2 and 3 for two views of the empire on the rise.)

Succession Planning. At the height of the Roman Empire, the emperor was not born to the role; he was chosen by the reigning emperor and "adopted." The most successful emperors-to-be also won buy-in from the military—a key constituency. The fittest successor benefited from a multiyear training program. The crowning years of the empire were marked by continuity of leadership that stretched from Caesar to Augustus to Tiberius. When Rome lost leadership continuity and military buy-in, it risked riots and civil wars.

Exhibit 2   **Rome Expands Through Organization, Infrastructure, and Leadership**

The Empire at Caesar's Death in 44 B.C.

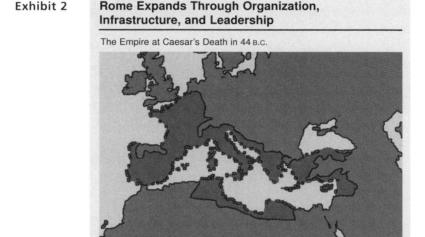

SOURCE: roman-empire.net, adapted with permission.

Exhibit 3 **Rome at Its Peak**

The Empire in A.D. 192

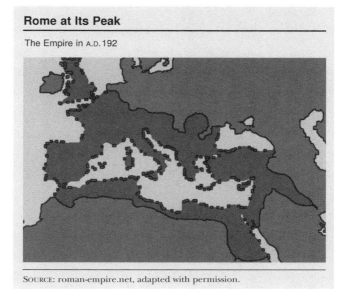

SOURCE: roman-empire.net, adapted with permission.

The Roman army was legendary for its strength, resilience, and flexibility. Loyalty and organization were built around the legion. Ten eight-man squads formed a century. There were six centuries to a cohort and ten cohorts to a full legion. The attack plan was organized in three lines. The first line was for the youngest soldiers, who were fierce, reckless, and brave. The second line was for experienced troops. The third rank was for the reserves. Defensive tactics dominated. Each squad had a well-defined role in every engagement. Each soldier understood his specific responsibilities and was an expert with his weapon. He knew his place in the line, and he knew what role he would take in the event of casualties in combat.

Organizational dogma provided the recipe for leadership and victory. Consider these rules left by an early Roman general:

1. Feed and rest the troops before battle.

2. Work them into a rage against the foe.

3. Take advantage of height.

4. Defend on rough ground.

5. In battle, engage with the sun behind you.

6.   Place the infantry in the center.

7.   Ensure adequate reserves.

8.   Concentrate force on breaking the enemy line.

9.   Provide an escape route.

10. Track down escapees with cavalry.

In their detailed manuals, the Roman leadership left little to chance.

Process Engineering to Deliver Productivity Advantage. Roman engineers broke tasks down into their simplest elements and recrafted projects so that everyone could make a contribution. By developing a series of steps into a process, the Romans achieved higher levels of productivity and improved quality.

The Roman model of government favored the professional manager—an arrangement that capitalized on the manager's experience and linked rewards to performance. At its height, Rome was managed by a cadre of fewer than 10,000 professional bureaucrats, chosen by merit, not patronage. The skills of the Roman machine were legendary, built around the need for long-range planning, logistics, campaign management, and infrastructure. Rome's managers honed the skills required to conscript, feed, and equip the world's largest army; collect progressive taxes; construct and transport weapons, building equipment, and other materials; and drive commerce.

At the peak of Roman influence, the emperor was highly visible, communicating with all citizens of the empire. The leader welcomed an honest confrontation with the truth. Virtuous, selfless behavior was rewarded. And the best emperors immediately responded to symptoms of trouble.

The Roman Empire created great wealth for those who served it. It was a very economically stratified society. The emperor Tiberius, the richest man in the first century, held an estate worth some $27 billion in real terms. Six men were ceded control of the whole African coast. This concentration of wealth permitted major capital projects, which further enhanced the strength and power of Rome.

Lessons from the Decline

There are, of course, many reasons for Rome's fall. Common to all is the fact that the emperors lost touch with what made the empire great and enabled it to prosper. The number one cause in our view was that the emperor was shielded from the truth.

Government was concentrated in the bureaucracy. In the last two centuries of the empire, power was for sale. You could buy a judgeship or a posting. The number of bureaucrats increased from 10,000 to 30,000. Discipline in the army became lax. The emperor did not seek a true understanding of the state of the union. The advantage in technology declined as the army went from 96 percent Roman to 3 percent. Citizens no longer viewed service in the army as a duty. Power shifted to the provinces. A decline in productivity caused wealth to evaporate and opened the door to civil war. At the same time, the emperors became increasingly caught in the trappings of power. No longer was the emperor the "first among citizens"; instead, he became robed, distant, and godlike.

We offer you this list of warning signs from the history of the Roman Empire, which we believe are applicable to modern times:

Instability. Rome suffered from political scheming and the failure to concentrate on growth.

Fragility of Advantage. As the Roman army shrank to a local militia, Rome's technology and scale became ineffective.

Lack of Strategic Reserves. Rome lived from year to year on annual crops and failed to provide mechanisms for savings. It also had no second line of defense beyond forts at the frontier.

Corruption. The behavior of Roman soldiers, officers, and public officials undercut edicts from headquarters.

Succession. Emperors began to be chosen by birth, not skill.

Few Impartial Metrics to Gauge Success. The Romans made no effort to maintain and balance productivity growth. They had few metrics to signal calamity before it spread, and they were willing to debase the currency.

In *The History of the Decline and Fall of the Roman Empire*, eighteenth-century historian Edward Gibbon brilliantly captured the empire's decline around A.D. 476:

> At the hour of midnight the Salerian gate was silently opened, and the inhabitants were awakened by the tremendous sound of the Gothic trumpet. Eleven hundred and sixty-three years after the foundation of Rome, the Imperial city, which had sub-

dued and civilised so considerable a part of mankind, was delivered to the licentious fury of the tribes of Germany and Scythia. (See Exhibit 4.)

Empires can, of course, still be created today. Let's look at The Home Depot, one of the world's greatest retail empires.

The Home Depot Rises in Two Decades

It has been only 20 years since The Home Depot issued its IPO. The Home Depot's empire was built on vision, courage, and economic advantage. Bernie Marcus, Arthur Blank, Ken Langone, and Pat Farrah devised the ultimate toy store for men, founded on a simple platform of lower prices, wider selection, and better, more knowledgeable service.

The Home Depot began as a chaotic, wild experiment. The first store's crew worked 48 hours straight to meet the aggressive opening deadline. On opening day, traffic was sparse. Advertising in the *Atlanta Constitution* promising lower prices and vast selection did not appear when expected. Two days later, when the ads finally hit, customers jammed the store to buy ceiling fans at unheard-of prices as well as inexpensive shovels, lumber, and light bulbs. Customers flocked to the store to ask for advice and learn. Sales asso-

Exhibit 4   **Outsiders Force Restructuring and Divestitures in the Face of Poor Management**

The Final Boundaries at the Last Emperor's Death in A.D.476

SOURCE: roman-empire.net, adapted with permission.

ciates were graded on their willingness to go the extra mile for the customer. It was trial by fire.

The business's proposition hinged on the conviction that The Home Depot would draw from a wider market and that lower prices would attract browsers as well as people interested in home improvement projects. As a result, the chain would be able to buy direct and save in sourcing.

The do-it-yourself revolution that The Home Depot created for the United States was radical and risky in 1981. Like the early Romans, The Home Depot provided prosperity for its loyal troops. It also inspired passion among its customers. In two decades, the company has grown to more than 1,100 stores and $50 billion in revenues. Vanquished in The Home Depot's wake are a variety of competitors: Builders Square, Hechinger's, Rickel, Handy Dan (the founders' former employer), Payless Cashways, and others. (See Exhibits 5 to 8.)

The Home Depot has created massive market value. In 1999, that value reached a peak of $158 billion. The Home Depot claims 1,000 millionaire employees among its ranks. This great business was built on an average of only $49 per transaction, a miserly 29.9 percent gross margin, and a 9.2 percent operating profit.

Exhibit 5	**The Home Depot Creates the Do-It-Yourself Category**

1979 sales:	$.007
1983 sales:	$.256
Ending market value:	$.658
Stores built:	19

SOURCES: BCG analysis; Home Depot annual reports.
NOTE: Dollar amounts are in billions.

Exhibit 6

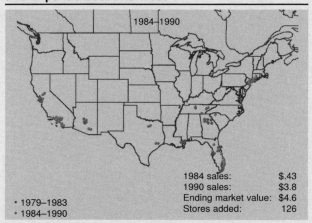

The Home Depot Builds Infrastructure and Expands East and West

1984–1990

1984 sales:	$.43
1990 sales:	$3.8
Ending market value:	$4.6
Stores added:	126

• 1979–1983
• 1984–1990

SOURCES: BCG analysis; Home Depot annual reports.
NOTE: Dollar amounts are in billions.

Exhibit 7

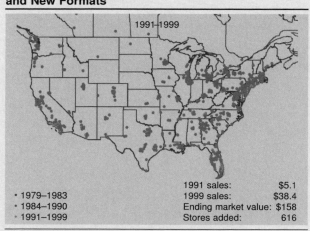

Further Expansion Through Acquisitions and New Formats

1991–1999

• 1979–1983
• 1984–1990
• 1991–1999

1991 sales:	$5.1
1999 sales:	$38.4
Ending market value:	$158
Stores added:	616

SOURCES: BCG analysis; Home Depot annual reports.
NOTE: Dollar amounts are in billions.

Exhibit 8

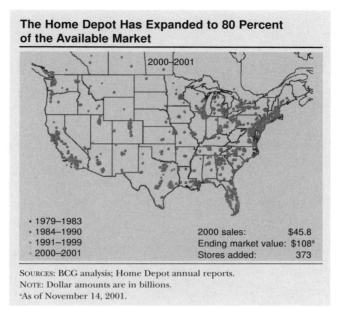

The Home Depot Has Expanded to 80 Percent of the Available Market

- 1979–1983
- 1984–1990
- 1991–1999
- 2000–2001

2000 sales:	$45.8
Ending market value:	$108[a]
Stores added:	373

SOURCES: BCG analysis; Home Depot annual reports.
NOTE: Dollar amounts are in billions.
[a]As of November 14, 2001.

Comparing the Rise of Rome to The Home Depot's Success

Like Rome, The Home Depot faces geographic limits (in its case, in the United States) as well as increasing competition, the mathematical burden of generating constant growth from an enormous base, and the challenge of maintaining the greatness of the founders' vision without those founders.

The Roman Empire suffered the strain of constant warfare, complacency, and disunity. It had a natural boundary around the Mediterranean basin. Increasingly, in later years, barbarian tribes encroached on multiple fronts. The empire became too large to manage and too large to achieve unity.

The Home Depot faces many similar challenges today. One of the company's keys to success was its initial hunger. The orange-aproned employee was urged never to lose a sale. Today the company has grown so large that it can no longer staff all of its stores with home improvement experts as it once did. The U.S. and Canadian markets are now largely served by The Home Depot and Lowe's superstores. Increasingly, The Home Depot finds itself fighting competitors on multiple fronts. It is at a turning point: complacency and decline down one path, renewal down the other.

At the beginning of this year, new leadership was appointed at The Home Depot. In effect, a new emperor was crowned. Bob Nardelli's challenge is to find growth, maintain momentum and spirit, and serve current customers well while continuing to expand. The Home Depot has announced that it will press to grow advantage in urban markets, delivered services, category extensions, and new locations. Nardelli brings experience and management talent from his years at industrial giant and financial services legend General Electric. One of his biggest tests will be to take a fantastically successful company to the next level of success.

Motivating associates and recruiting talented people are probably the toughest challenges for The Home Depot and for all of us. Employees appropriately seek inspiration, recognition, mobility, and impact. As our companies grow, the leadership must maintain connections, clarity of purpose, and a continuous stream of intelligence. It must also retain talented employees and foster a culture of rewarding performance.

Antennae Aimed and Ready to Receive External Input

In our business world, if we are to defeat the enemies of success, we must challenge the prevailing wisdom. That requires us to gather new facts about consumers' hopes and dreams, competitors' threats, and our resulting options. It requires insight into the right path and interactions that mobilize the organization. And, most important, it requires the courage to take on this challenge at the very peak of success.

Over the past ten years, many consumer packaged-goods and retail companies have created significant value by innovating, investing preemptively, improving early advantage, and picking the right successor at the right time.

Wal-Mart has created nearly $200 billion in shareholder value, and The Home Depot has generated more than $100 billion of wealth. PepsiCo has created more than $40 billion in wealth by focusing on and growing its beverage and snack food businesses, and by shedding its bottling operations and restaurants. Dayton Hudson Corporation, renamed Target Corporation, has generated $30 billion in wealth by abandoning its role as a leader in department stores and becoming a leader in upscale discount stores.

However, other companies have underperformed the market and remain stuck as "mature" businesses. Over the next ten years, will your company create value by allowing a great idea to mature or will it create value through rejuvenation?

Please make our year-end homily relevant to your business by considering these questions:

1. Can you check off the winning elements of Roman history and The Home Depot's story that reside in your company?

2. Can you complete a diagnostic on your company, identifying the symptoms and likely causes of possible decline?

3. Can you describe and communicate your plan to halt any decline and return to a greatness based on new sources of advantage and a cross-business, customer-centered view of your next opportunity for revolution?

This article was first published in December 2001.

Pricing with Precision and Impact

Jacques Chapuis, Michael Haugen, Orin Herskowitz, and Roy Lowrance

Of all the tools companies can use to spur consumers to act, pricing is often the most effective—but also the most blunt. Few companies think they are earning the highest profits possible from their price promotions or even their basic prices. But that's changing. Recent advances in information technology have greatly sharpened the pricing tool, permitting ever finer consumer segmentation. The technology has done this in two ways. It has dramatically expanded the breadth and depth of information about consumers that companies can gather and process, and it has made possible the instantaneous delivery of customized pricing offers to individual consumers.

Taken together, these advances signal an end to the era of broadly averaged, one-size-fits-many pricing and herald the dawn of truly price-differentiated commerce. The impact on businesses, business models, and consumers stands to be nothing less than profound.

To be sure, the promise of differentiated or individualized pricing is hardly new. Getting consumers to haggle, bid, or otherwise actively work to win incremental savings was central to the business model of many a failed "dynamic pricing" dot-com. What has changed, however, is that more subtle ways of collecting data and transmitting offers are allowing dynamic pricing to occur in the background, unseen and unbidden by the consumer. These new technologies make receiving individualized prices effortless and ultra-convenient for consumers. The resulting opportunities for businesses are powerful, provable, and immediate.

Most companies, however, are ill prepared for this new world. Their strategies and daily operations have long been predicated on averaged pricing, in which one group of customers effectively subsidizes another. When it becomes possible to deliver individually segmented offers, prices will become de-averaged, and customer subsidies will disappear. Companies that aren't ready for the transition could find themselves victims of "cream skimming," as their best customers are lured away and the average costs to serve their remaining customers increase.

Preparing for this radically altered landscape is not simply a matter of understanding and implementing the best technology. Companies will also need to shift their thinking and initiate changes at all levels of the business. They will be forced to deal with their customers' confusion and apprehension, and they should anticipate government regulation.

But companies have little choice. De-averaged pricing is real. For many businesses, it is just around the corner; for some it is already here.

The Pricing Process

There are two primary steps in the pricing process: the gathering and analyzing of data about consumers and the communicating of an appropriate offer. Recent advances in technology have greatly enhanced the ability to execute both steps.

Gathering and Analyzing Data. Technology is giving companies an increasingly subtle, yet more and more potent, arsenal of ways to collect consumer data. These fall under two headings: active and passive. Active data collection occurs when consumers provide personal data in exchange for information or services. Pepsi and Marlboro, for example, offer branded merchandise to customers who amass a certain number of "points" and sign up for membership in a program that requires them to provide personal information. The companies can then identify the most loyal customers and track their behavior.

Passive collection occurs when the underlying technology itself provides the information—without consumers' active participation. Besides opening new avenues of data gathering, it can also yield more accurate information, precisely because it does not rely on consumers' active involvement. (People often err or exaggerate when they volunteer personal information.) Such technologies as GPS (Global Positioning System) and cell-tower triangulation allow for ready determination of consumers' locations. "Screen scraping" and other browser-tracking technologies make it possible for companies to collect data about demand and price sensitivity even before consumers make a purchase. And thanks to telematics, a technology that uses chips embedded in products to transmit information, manufacturers can collect data on product use directly and in real time.

These new capabilities give companies two major advantages they did not enjoy before. First, with access to data about actual consumers' identity, location, usage, and demand in advance of purchasing decisions, companies can reverse the cycle of the traditional pricing process. Rather than being forced to set a price and then determine its popularity, companies can now gauge a consumer's likely price threshold with a high degree of confidence before making a pricing offer.

Second, thanks to data-mining software and powerful eCRM (electronic customer-relationship management) systems, companies are learning how to organize and analyze their enormous collections of customer data in a manner that previously would have been cost prohibitive, if not impossible. With this capability, companies can define and segment markets on the basis of any number or combination of criteria rather than simply by such broad factors as zip codes and demographic details. The still evolving ability to define ever narrower segments, including, ultimately, "segments of one," is an advance with powerful implications.

Designing and Making Pricing Offers. Advances in technology are also revolutionizing the second half of the pricing equation: the delivery of the offer itself.

The most exciting development is the advent of individualized delivery. Having rich information about specific customers is useful only if companies can tailor and deliver pricing offers to those customers individually, without risking the cannibalization of other customers. This capability is finally arriving. Internet cookies and personal wireless devices allow companies to deliver a specific price at a specific time to a specific customer—and to that customer only. Cell phones facilitate this exclusivity by not permitting users to forward individualized offers to friends. Furthermore, the digital nature of these media lower the "menu costs" associated with frequently changing posted prices, allowing for a greater range of pricing possibilities.

Businesses can also create and deliver pricing offers in response to an increasingly wide array of "triggers." A company can design and offer a price to an individual on the basis of his or her identity and usage patterns or on a combination of facts that are unique to a particular moment: the person is within 400 yards of a certain store, has a history of purchasing products from that store, and has recently completed a Web search for products the store carries. This capability will become especially powerful as passive data collection becomes pervasive, courtesy of ever cheaper and smaller chip-based transmitting devices.

Early Movers

Consumer companies are already beginning to exploit these new capabilities. For example, a national retailer captures data on new customers who use branded credit cards and identifies those individuals whose profiles match the company's targeted consumer segments. It then turns these new shoppers into loyal customers by offering them deep discounts on products that are most likely to interest them. Using similar technology, a supermarket chain identifies customers who respond strongly to price discounts on a particular item and offers them a permanent "coupon" for that product whenever they show their loyalty card at checkout.

New technology can also identify the right price for each item. ShopKo, a discount retail chain in the United States, recently piloted markdown software that helps it determine precisely which items to discount, when, where, and by how much. Making sense of unwieldy amounts of data from individual stores, the software develops recommendations on the basis of how quickly the product category is expected to sell in each store. The recommendations incorporate such factors as pricing elasticity and the number of weeks or months until the product will go out of date for seasonal or other reasons. The technology, which can account for changes in buying patterns across a small geographic area, even suggests different discounts for a single item being sold in several stores around town. So far, the program has been a success: the gross margin is up 24 percent on test merchandise.

Of course, these capabilities aren't limited to retailers. An auto service company, for instance, could offer discounts on oil changes or tune-ups on the basis of customers' frequency of purchase. The discounts might even be offered through customers' cell phones or directly through their cars' onboard computers.

As the cost of technology decreases, product and service providers could also insert intelligence into the product itself. For instance, prices for cell-phone service vary widely because providers track customers' usage patterns and group them by similar behaviors in order to maximize the value of the service to both customer and provider. Each group has a different pricing structure so that customers can select the structure that most closely matches their expected needs. Soon, other "dumb" devices, such as home appliances, autos, and cable television, will carry technology that tracks consumers' behavior and allows for individualized pricing.

Another intriguing example is SCAN, a provider of cellular-based price-comparison technology in the United States and the United Kingdom. With SCAN's service, a consumer in a bricks-and-mortar store can access information about a product by entering its name or Universal Product Code into a cell phone. SCAN responds instantly, sending price information from competing online and offline retailers, as well as the means to order the product directly from those retailers. The company plans eventually to track consumers' locations, browsing patterns, and purchasing histories, including the degree to which promotional discounts appear to drive purchasing decisions.

Turning Promise into Advantage

As the technology continues to evolve, the transition to individualized pricing will only accelerate. Companies should therefore begin to think seriously about how to position themselves at the front of the curve. Here are some initial steps they might consider taking:

Think "big picture." A company must anticipate the threats and opportunities inherent in its current pricing structure. It needs to determine which of its customers are subsidizing others and consider ways that it—or a competitor—might exploit the underlying pricing disparities. Otherwise, it could well see its best customers become ex-customers.

Embrace the right technology. Companies must quickly bring themselves up to speed on the full spectrum of technologies, identifying those that might add value to their businesses. In particular, they should examine technologies that facilitate the collection and analysis of customer data and the delivery of individualized pricing offers. They should also be aware of current or emerging technological standards that could affect their choice of equipment and partners.

Plan for broad operational changes. Companies should recognize that they will need to upgrade systems and processes for both speed and interoperability. Many functions that are now performed manually—including the determination of when to change prices—will need to be automated. Companies should start drawing a project map for this makeover.

Prepare customers. As Amazon discovered recently, some resistance from customers to individualized pricing—particularly to perceived pricing inequities—is inevitable. During what Amazon described as a "random" pricing experiment, the company appeared to be penalizing some of its loyal customers with higher prices, causing an uproar that was settled only with Amazon's making apologies and giving refunds.

Companies need to recognize that customers' apprehensions about unfair pricing, as well as their growing worries about privacy, are valid. Retailers should have clear mission statements that explain the pricing logic or criteria they use to differentiate customers. The statements should also spell out plans for handling sensitive customer data. To further assuage consumers' concerns and to ensure their willing participation, companies should begin to educate their current customers about the potential benefits of individualized pricing—including convenience and the ability to "earn" better prices.

Anticipate regulatory hurdles. Given consumers' worries about privacy and fairness, and the fact that individualized pricing will indeed lead to higher prices for some consumers, government intervention is also a certainty. Companies may ultimately have little say here. Still, they need to be aware of the ways in which pending regulation could speed or slow the adoption of new pricing strategies in their industries.

Count on a bumpy ride. Individualized pricing will be dynamic in more than one way. Because technology will continue to evolve, companies must prepare for new twists and turns as the rules of the game also evolve. For example, it is likely that technologies that can capture individualized pricing offers and then broadcast them to interested consumers will emerge. It is also likely that consumers will eventually have the means to block unwanted collection of data. All the more reason to begin educating them now.

*   *   *

The technology-driven shift from averaged to individualized pricing, already under way, will be seismic in scope. For some companies, it will mean a material boost to their business and their ability to attract new customers; for others, the consequences could be harsh. But the genie is out of the bottle. Companies can substantially increase their chances of success in this new environment by planning for the transition now, while the competitive landscape is still open.

This article was first published in January 2002.

Competitive Advantage from Mobile Applications

Joe Manget

The mobile commerce revolution, heralded periodically since the late 1990s, has yet to occur in most retail markets. Consumers have shied away from increasingly complex handsets and from bandwidths that are still too slow. As a result, predictions of huge retail profits from m-commerce remain unfulfilled. Yet inside the supply chains of many cutting-edge retailers and their partners, a true mobile revolution has begun. Consumer-focused companies are already using wireless technology to get closer to their customers and improve their efficiency by cutting cycle times and costs.

Nearly three-quarters of the top 40 retailers in the United States have deployed or tested at least one wireless application, although only 10 percent are offering consumer applications. (See Exhibit 1.) We expect wireless business applications to grow twice as fast as consumer applications: supply chain applications are quickly becoming a requirement for every company. Yet businesses can still differentiate themselves through improved consumer applications.

Organizations that have embraced relatively simple wireless tools for sales force automation or customer relationship management have seen productivity gains ranging from 5 to 30 percent. PepsiCo/Frito-Lay, FedEx, and UPS mobilized distribution processes for a cost savings of 10 to 20 percent thanks to productivity gains, increased asset visibility, and improved decision-making capabilities. The Home Depot is saving $22 million a year by providing floor employees with the ability to check and order inventory using wireless technology.

Exhibit 1   **Most Top Retailers Use Wireless Applications**

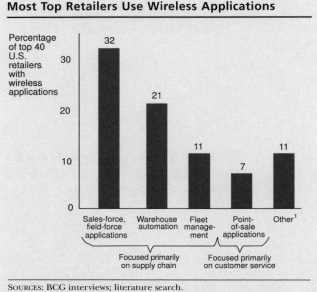

SOURCES: BCG interviews; literature search.
NOTE: Some companies use more than one type of application.
[1]Includes electronic signage, wireless shelf-tag pricing, and wireless online prescriptions at pharmacies.

How the Development of Applications Will Unfold

As consumer companies embrace wireless applications, three significant stages of development will occur. First, communication between organizations and their employees, customers, and suppliers will be radically enhanced, in effect mobilizing business operations. Second, companies will use new data from consumers and equipment to reshape business models. And third, previously untapped data will be processed in ways that will change the rules of competition and even redefine industries. (See Exhibit 2.)

Business operations will be mobilized. To date, most wireless activity within organizations has accelerated and simplified communication with field employees, suppliers, and customers—thereby enhancing existing business processes. Office Depot, for example, is using wireless technology to reduce operating costs and improve customer service. Fleet drivers are given a PDA with an embedded bar-code scanner to read each delivery item as it is loaded onto the truck. That information, along with the truck's location en route, is transmitted wirelessly to the company's back-office systems, automatically

Exhibit 2

Increasing Opportunities for Wireless Applications

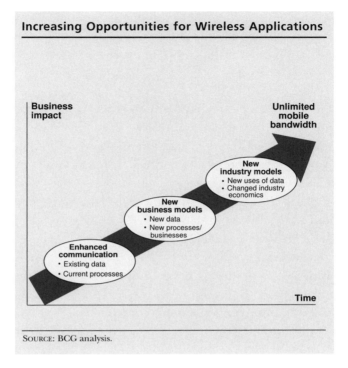

SOURCE: BCG analysis.

creating a manifest that's viewable on the company's Web site. Upon delivery, payment can be processed remotely and signatures captured electronically, eliminating millions of dollars in costs per year from reconciliation errors.

Other leading companies have found creative ways to employ wireless applications:

- Federated Department Stores is testing electronic-ink solutions to reduce the $250,000 it spends every month manually changing its signage. Now, through a radio connection, an operator can make tiny two-sided balls embedded within paper flip to their black or white sides to form letters.

- Sears, Roebuck has transformed the mobility of its 15,000 sales associates into a competitive advantage by equipping them with hand-held devices connected to wireless LANs in its 860 mall stores. This technology has enabled associates to check and change prices, receive inventory, and even print pricing labels.

- To eliminate long checkout lines, The Home Depot is piloting a wireless point-of-sale program in which roaming cashiers process transactions right at the shopping cart for customers paying with credit or debit cards.

These companies are not just benefiting from better customer service, streamlined operations, and improved pricing accuracy. Their use of wireless technology is also preparing them for the day when customers will make mobile payments or simply beam their wish lists and contact information to a sales associate.

Of course, retailers aren't the only consumer businesses to benefit from wireless technology. Nabisco uses a wireless LAN in its warehouses and provides staff with a portable, voice-directed computer that is linked to a bar-code-scanning inventory system. Picking speeds have improved by 12 percent, with a measurable increase in quality. At Frito-Lay, mobile sales reps can update order information wirelessly at the retailer, thereby reducing stockouts and improving inventory control. Orders are now processed up to seven hours earlier than they were in the past, and trucks are loaded five hours earlier.

Business models will be reshaped. The second wave of wireless applications, now starting to appear, promises to be more far-reaching than the first. Rather than merely accelerating or improving information flows, these applications will also drive changes in an organization's core processes and pave the way for fundamentally new business models.

In Japan, for example, NTT DoCoMo has partnered with vending-machine manufacturers and soft-drink companies to equip vending machines with wireless capability. In addition to accepting payments from wireless devices, the machines use wireless technology to transmit information on inventory levels and maintenance problems. Beverage companies use perishable data such as information on point-of-sale inventory—information that could not be captured previously—to improve distribution and product selection, and reduce the number of out-of-stock items. Those moves have increased profits per machine by as much as 70 percent.

The rules of competition will change. As businesses capture and process remote data from a greater variety of sources, some will find opportunities to revamp their cost structures, increase market share, and even create new ways of competing. Progressive Casualty Insurance Company, a U.S. auto insurer, provides an intriguing example. It is piloting a new underwriting system that uses wireless technology to track customer behavior behind the wheel. By equipping cars with relatively low-cost locating devices, Progressive collects information such as where individuals drive, how fast, how often, and when, as well as where they park. It uses the information to price monthly premiums on the basis of specific usage, not actuarial data. Over time, drivers with good records and few claims are likely to remain with Progressive, whereas higher-risk drivers may move to other insurers. If this system is implemented on a large scale, it could change the face of the auto insurance industry.

A Call to Action

In the excitement over the future of m-commerce, many companies are forgetting that real opportunities are available today that can significantly improve their competitive position. Although a surprising number of retailers and consumer goods companies are advanced in mobile technology, most have failed to realize the full potential of wireless. It's not too late to capture the benefits or to develop new business and industry models for long-term gains.

Companies that have yet to use wireless technology should immediately begin to screen opportunities for wireless applications in order to improve in-stock rates, promotional modeling, sales force productivity, and the exchange of supply-chain information. To decide whether a given business area will benefit from wireless technology, a company must determine whether it has the right combination of mobile employees, remote goods and equipment, and perishable or dynamic data—and whether the technology will have a significant impact on the business. (See Exhibit 3.)

We recommend the following four-step process to get started:

Develop m-awareness. Begin a campaign to help the organization understand all that m-commerce can do. Then build a network of people committed to meeting the challenge of implementation.

Generate ideas for realizing the goal. Assign a team to lay out the business system and potential opportunities. Then formalize the ideas into initiatives to be investigated further and track each of them.

Conduct m-triage. Develop a business case for each initiative and evaluate it on its potential to attract additional revenues, reduce costs, unlock opportunities, and offer strategic advantage. Then prioritize your initiatives,

Exhibit 3   **Determine Where Wireless Applications Will Offer the Best Opportunities**

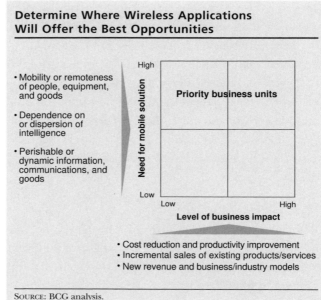

SOURCE: BCG analysis.

identifying those you want to pursue immediately, those that need further study, and those you will shelve.

Don't delay in launching wireless initiatives. Start with the projects that are easy to execute—messaging, e-mail, dynamic scheduling—and focus on customer-oriented initiatives. Then add the new generation of mobile applications. Partner with mobile suppliers and form joint ventures. Tie it all to your logistics network, customize it, fine-tune the interface, and get ready for unlimited mobile bandwidth.

Few truly wireless companies exist today. Yet the technology can provide companies with improved productivity, lower costs, and more control over the supply chain. If you do the spadework and become m-enabled, you will reap benefits when the m-commerce revolution finally arrives. Get ahead of your competitors and lay the groundwork for a world that will be connected, informed, and rich with data.

This article was first published in February 2002.

Strategic E-Triage: Identifying Essential E-Business Initiatives

Katrina Helmkamp and Neil Monnery

E-business has been overhyped. Wise companies will cut budgeted investments sharply.

E-business will transform relationships between companies and their customers, suppliers, and employees. It will revolutionize competition.

Which of these statements do you believe? Probably, like us, you think both are true. That's what makes setting the direction for e-businesses so difficult. In an effort to slash expenses and boost profitability, consumer companies are writing off many of the e-business initiatives they approved during the past three years. Usually, however, they embark on this exercise without a clear sense of which projects to kill and which to keep. As a result, most companies will overreact and cut too deeply.

The Boston Consulting Group's work with clients confirms that many companies can prudently reduce e-business expenses by as much as half. That's not to say that some of their remaining initiatives don't offer real opportunities. To give a new twist to the old proverb "All that glitters is not gold": All that is "e" is not dead.

Indeed, consumers have widely adopted the Internet as a vehicle to seek information about various products. They use search engines with ease and are increasingly turning to the Internet for books, music, computers, software, and travel. (See Exhibit 1.) Online purchases in 2001 reached nearly $60 billion—up from $44.5 billion in 2000.

Exhibit 1

Online Buying Has Increased in All Categories

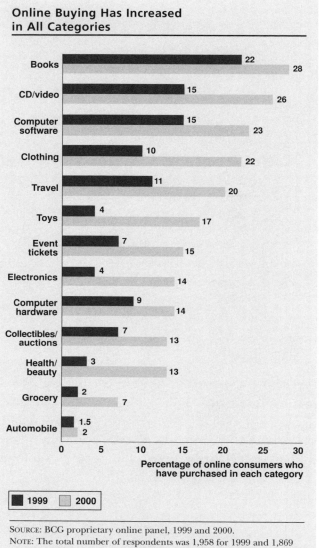

Percentage of online consumers who have purchased in each category

■ 1999   ▢ 2000

SOURCE: BCG proprietary online panel, 1999 and 2000.
NOTE: The total number of respondents was 1,958 for 1999 and 1,869 for 2000.

In our client work, we've found that almost every consumer company has two or three e-business projects that are well worth continued investment. If managers can integrate those projects into core processes, they can generate significant incremental profits. Here are some examples of companies that did just that:

- Low-cost airlines have further extended their advantage by obliterating their distribution costs. In Europe, companies such as easyJet have built a cost advantage of several hundred basis points over traditional airlines through their low-cost Internet-based booking systems.

- Procter & Gamble has learned how to use the Web to cut its advertising costs. It developed a site for dentists and offered them an 800 number to build critical mass for its Whitestrips tooth whitener before launching it in retail stores. The success with early adopters encouraged the company to launch the product with minimal advertising. The experiment paid off: after just six weeks, Whitestrips hit its sales target for the entire year.

- BMW leveraged the Internet to increase brand awareness among targeted high-income consumers. During the past year, several million people visited bmwfilms.com to see a series of edgy short movies, spending an average of 11 minutes at the site. A television advertising campaign drawing equal exposure would have cost $20 million to $25 million more than BMW spent on the site.

- A grocery retailer used its frequent-shopper transaction data to better target its promotional offers and saved 1 percent of sales.

- Both Kraft Foods and Campbell Soup Company built valuable relationships with their heavy users through permission-based marketing of recipes and tips on the Internet.

- Unilever estimates that its e-business will deliver revenue and cost benefits equal to 2 percent of sales.

Some of these initiatives push profits up in the short term but are quickly copied by competitors. Others create genuine, sustainable advantage, and those are the ones that will change the competitive landscape over the next decade. But managers face a ticklish problem. It takes a while for shifts in advantage to show up in relative profitability, particularly since innovators tend to invest heavily in growth, making their profitability appear artificially low in the early years. That being the case, how can managers pursue the short-term opportunity to reduce costs in e-business activities without destroying necessary investments to sustain and build longer-term competitive advantage? Both agendas are valid and must be acted on. Yet in a world of simplistic sound bites, it's all too easy to lose sight of the subtle complexity of a company's real needs.

In our work with consumer companies, we have seen enormous benefit accrue to those that use a strategic e-triage approach to evaluating e-business investments. The process is straightforward and entails the three steps described below.

Step 1. Audit All E-Business Initiatives

The first step is to compile a detailed inventory of every e-business project in the company. That means gathering such information as who is in charge of each project, what resources are involved, the original rationale for investment, and the results to date.

Once a company begins this process, it usually discovers many more initiatives than it expected to find, some without even a rudimentary business case. Project proliferation often happens in companies that operate through geographic subsidiaries—with each region likely to have its own initiatives—as well as in companies that have separate "czars" for business-to-business, business-to-consumer, and business-to-employee projects. Most companies find that they have 30 to 75 initiatives. The goal is to end up with a focused list of no more than 10. (See Exhibit 2.)

Exhibit 2

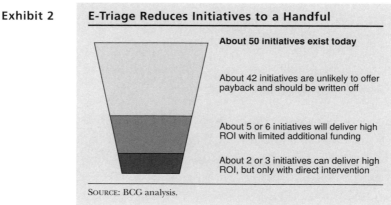

E-Triage Reduces Initiatives to a Handful

About 50 initiatives exist today

About 42 initiatives are unlikely to offer payback and should be written off

About 5 or 6 initiatives will deliver high ROI with limited additional funding

About 2 or 3 initiatives can deliver high ROI, but only with direct intervention

SOURCE: BCG analysis.

Step 2. Estimate the Opportunity for Each Initiative

Before the list can be winnowed, the business potential of each initiative must be assessed. We recommend linking each project to specific business processes, such as supply chain management. This pegs the project to concrete, measurable objectives—revenue growth, cost reduction, or efficiency improvements—and provides it with a clear "owner" to judge it. (See Exhibit 3.) Then you can work with the owner to understand the expected financial impact. For many initiatives, benchmarks and pilot results are available to evaluate business cases, and if tailored to the specific environment, they can help generate good estimates. Working with the line manager responsible for an area or process should also reduce double-counting or undue optimism.

Beyond the direct financial expectations, you also need to assess whether the initiative will have an impact on competitive advantage. Is there a first-mover advantage? Is there a chance to lock in key suppliers or customers and raise switching costs? Is there scale to be exploited? Could you create capabilities that are hard to replicate? Is the advantage sustainable or is it easy to copy?

Exhibit 3

Link Each E-Business Initiative to Measurable Objectives

E-Business Initiative	Measurable Objectives
E-procurement	Reduction in direct-materials costs and purchasing transaction costs
Collaborative planning, forecasting, and replenishment	Reduction in inventory carrying costs and stockouts
Collaborative new-product development	Increase in the number of innovative projects and in speed to market for new products
Customer relationship management	Increase in cross-selling (measured by average purchase or number of categories purchased) and customer retention
Knowledge management	Increase in employee satisfaction and retention; decrease in the amount of time it takes to resolve a customer's problem
Employee benefits	Decrease in the amount of time it takes for employees to change addresses and update benefits

SOURCE: BCG experience.

Step 3. Develop a Framework for Setting Priorities

Once a company has identified all its e-business initiatives and assessed their potential, it is ready to develop a framework for deciding which projects are worth continuing and under what conditions. Of course, projects that generate high returns would warrant top priority and, perhaps, further investment. Indeed, one of the main benefits of cutting investment elsewhere is often the opportunity to increase it here.

Projects that are likely to generate high returns but offer little competitive advantage might assume the follower's position, adopting the best tactics of competitors as quickly as possible. That makes it easier to bring a tested system in-house and limits the drain on scarce internal resources. It also helps strengthen a company's skills at being an effective fast follower.

If the initiative creates a lot of advantage but depresses short-term returns, that is a real tradeoff. Is there a way to explain the advantage to investors? Is there a way to cut costs by working with an outside partner—without losing the advantage? If there is no way around the tradeoff, then it's advisable to fund only the best of such opportunities and carefully manage the complex tradeoffs they present.

Exhibit 4 shows one framework that BCG uses with many different kinds of companies to help them prioritize their e-business initiatives. A packaged-goods manufacturer, for instance, placed e-procurement in its first-priority quadrant because low costs were critical to its market position. It worked closely with FreeMarkets' auction system to reduce the cost of its direct materials by a staggering 8 percent. It also established customized interfaces with many of its suppliers to trim 15 percent from the transaction costs of purchasing.

Another manufacturer, whose products tend to be impulse purchases, put collaborative planning, forecasting, and replenishment (CPFR) in its first quadrant and immediately began to exchange information with its key retailers to reduce stockouts. That provided a 20 percent sales lift. But, unlike the first manufacturer, it gave e-procurement second priority because it was content to move more slowly in that area. Consequently, it worked with established systems on its noncommodity inputs and refrained from committing IT resources to customized solutions. Nevertheless, it captured an incremental 2 percent savings on its direct-materials costs—enough to remain competitive in that area.

Exhibit 4

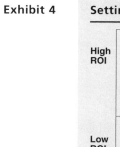

Setting Priorities for E-Business Initiatives

	Low alignment with strategy/does not create advantage	**High alignment with strategy/creates advantage**
High ROI	**Priority 2** Be a fast follower in these initiatives—no customized solutions	**Priority 1** Invest in these initiatives, even if they require customization
Low ROI	**Priority 4** Stop all activity on these initiatives and reallocate resources	**Priority 3** Reduce costs (consolidate into global effort, work with partners)

SOURCE: BCG experience.

Interestingly, initiatives that ended up in the fourth quadrant—whether the client was a service company, retailer, or manufacturer—often turned out to be driven by the IT department, with little or no strategic input from the business units. Because our matrix is grounded in a company's individual strategy and supported with hard data, it permits a clear and precise view of where crucial resources could be freed up from low-priority initiatives and moved to higher-priority ones.

To conduct a quick audit of your e-business initiatives, consider the following questions:

- How many e-business initiatives are really operating inside our company?

- How many of them are supported by a business case and an estimated return on investment?

- Do we know which initiatives are critical for competitive advantage and which could be fast followers? Are our IT resources aligned accordingly?

- Does each initiative have a senior owner? Is that owner working to integrate the initiative into our core business processes?

- Does senior management receive updates on progress every quarter?

- Do we routinely stop initiatives that offer little in returns or competitive advantage?

The Role of Top Management

Periods of change are always the most exciting time to be a senior manager. And the most dangerous. In the last few years, we have gone from regarding the Internet with skepticism to a period of unbridled optimism and then to skepticism again. Yet despite this emotional roller coaster, the technology continues to advance day by day, year by year. Many of us will get caught up in the exciting swings because they create fascinating stories. But the more important story is the long-term silent shift in advantage.

For senior managers, now is the time to make those difficult tradeoffs between the short term and the long term, and to allocate the company's resources to create advantage. Like so many strategic issues, e-triage is worth the time and effort because the short-term ups and downs of the stock market and the shifting views of the media are often very poor guides.

This article was first published in March 2002.

Trading Up: The New Luxury and Why We Need It

Neil Fiske and Michael Silverstein

In the history of man, there have always been goods reserved for the upper classes. In ancient Rome, the elite built lavish marble baths for entertaining friends and allies, while the masses waited in line at public baths. In late-eighteenth-century France, the aristocracy turned to saddle maker Hermès for the perfect seat, while commoners had to walk through wet and muddy streets.

But today we are witnessing a different phenomenon: the democratization of luxury. We define it as middle-market consumers selectively trading up to higher levels of quality, taste, and aspiration.

The democratization of luxury is occurring across a surprisingly broad set of categories, and it is destabilizing competition, creating new winners and losers, and offering new rules for brand strategy. Already, this force has transformed a score of markets. (See Exhibit 1.) Many more categories are ripe for the taking. The question for established marketers is, Who will be first to bring the new luxury to my category?

To understand this movement, you must first appreciate the differences between the new luxury and the old, as well as the powerful emotional and economic forces behind consumers' propensity to trade up and seek quality.

It's Not Your Father's Luxury

Old luxury is expensive. Only the really rich—a small segment, typically over 50 and conservative—can afford it. The new luxury democratizes high-quality products, making them available in many forms, at many price lev-

Exhibit 1   **The New-Luxury Revolution Cuts Across Many Categories**

Coffee	Starbucks
Personal care	Bath & Body Works, Origins, "masstige" products
Oral care	Rembrandt, Crest Whitestrips, Sonicare, and other appliances
Appliances	Sub-Zero, Viking
Home	Martha Stewart, Williams-Sonoma, Crate and Barrel, The Home Depot, The Great Indoors
Food	Gourmet frozen pizza, ice cream, and ready-to-mix greens
Wine	Robert Mondavi, Kendall Jackson
Lingerie	Victoria's Secret
Automobiles	Lexus, Mercedes-Benz, BMW, Porsche
Pet food	Eagle Pack, Bil-Jac, Diamond
Spas	A $5 billion industry, growing 25% annually
Toys	American Girl
Sporting goods	Callaway (golf), Nike (basketball shoes)
Beverages	SoBe, Danone, enhanced water
Chocolate	Godiva, Ferrero Rocher
Restaurants	Panera Bread, Outback Steakhouse, The Cheesecake Factory
Electronics	Home theater, HDTV, DVDs, Bang & Olufsen

Source: BCG analysis.

els, and through a variety of retail channels; they are no longer confined to the upscale shops of Madison Avenue and Rodeo Drive. New luxury is so accessible that virtually anyone can get a taste of it with a $3 Starbucks latte and a few moments in an inviting chair. It's less about conspicuous consumption and more about self-respect and emotional need.

New luxury is also more resilient. While exclusive luxury declined sharply in the recession of 2001, new luxury showed its staying power. The fault lines between the old and the new luxury became clear. Tiffany was down, but Starbucks sales grew 20 percent, and comparable store sales continued to rise. Panera Bread, an upscale bakery and quick-service restaurant chain, grew more than 50 percent to over $500 million, with 6 percent growth in comp store sales. Premium chocolate, an affordable luxury in a down market, grew 10 to 15 percent—two to three times the rate of the overall market. And dark chocolate—the richer, more sophisticated choice—grew to 27 percent of the category from just 20 percent a few years ago. Sales of single-serve bottled water increased more than 30 percent and continued to grow with increasing variety and next-generation enhancements. (See Exhibit 2.)

Victoria's Secret had a strong holiday performance, as did Williams-Sonoma. Longing for the emotional comforts of home, consumers bought higher-end appliances at a surprising rate. The fastest-growing market in consumer electronics for three years running is home theater, where entry-level systems start at $2,000 and the high end begins at $100,000.

The differences between the old and the new luxury become even clearer when you look closely at both the consumers and the providers. The buyers of new luxury are not slaves to brands. They are fiercely loyal *when they choose to be*, but they are also discriminating and know their needs. As brand apostles, they are a marketer's dream. They care about the brand's history,

Exhibit 2   **Enhanced Bottled Waters Are Entering the Market**

Gatorade Propel Fitness Water
"Vitamin charged"

Aquéss
"Delivers 20% of daily fiber requirements as recommended by AHA"

Aqua Clara
"800% more pure oxygen than ordinary water"

Peace Mountain Heart Smart Magnesium Mineral Water
"Give your heart a healthy start"

Glacéau Water
"Fluid embodiment of physical and spiritual well-being"

Penta-Hydrate Oxygenated Water
"The next generation of water"

Hansen's E$_2$0 Energy Water
"Infused with energy-boosting ingredients"

Looney Tunes Fortified Spring Water (for kids)
"With fluoride and calcium"

SOURCES: Company Web sites; bevnet.com.

romance its "heritage," and urge their friends to try it, just once. The buyers of new luxury form intellectual, emotional, and even spiritual attachments to products and brands.

To afford their new-luxury preferences, consumers are economizing across a wide swath of their purchases, using quality and value as their guides. More than ever, they are simultaneously trading up and trading down. A sophisticated shopper will recognize a bargain in a well-made knit top on promotion at Target for only $10 and then spend $500 on a Gucci handbag. She has the cash and will pay the price.

What the middle-market consumer will not do is fall for mediocrity. She wants quality at all price points and—by selectively reaching for better brands—has become more discerning and more demanding.

From the supply side, the sellers of new luxury are genuine innovators and entrepreneurs who bring vision and imagination to products and services that have become either expensive and stale or cheap and undifferentiated. These innovators tend to be industry outsiders who take advantage of their freedom from category dogma to imagine a brand that offers more emotional resonance, higher quality, a superior experience, and better economics. They are expert, authentic, and authoritative in every detail. Their product-launch model is different, and they seek out and find visible apostles. They use the resulting mystique to drive loyalty and repurchase. They are masters at segmentation, particularly along emotional dimensions. Unfortunately, the vast majority of current category participants are turning a deaf ear to the new-luxury trend, and by the time they notice it, it may be too late.

Because They're Worth It

Consider pet food. Dogs and cats throughout North America and Europe are enjoying designer dinners specially formulated for their age, breed, lifestyle, and particular dietary needs. The food is attractively packaged, smells good (even to humans), and tastes delicious (or so the animals' hearty consumption suggests). The pet owners who buy premium food do so because it doesn't cost *that* much more, because they believe it's better for their pets, and because they treat their pets like family members.

In recent years, the overall pet-food market in the United States has been growing at approximately 2 percent, with thin—6 to 9 percent—operating margins that are typical in commodity pricing. Stalemate strategies have prevailed, and several of the larger players have merged. But the prognosis looks much better for the companies that have discovered the affordable luxury market, such as Diamond Pet Foods, Eagle Pack, and Bil-Jac Foods. Those companies are growing at 10 percent per year, with operating margins two to three times the industry average. Today the premium segment represents about 20 percent of category sales but half of profits.

The idea of lavishing so much attention on pets may seem like typical yuppie excess, but the new luxury isn't a branding gimmick. The gourmet-pet-food companies have significantly revamped the product and its delivery, while tapping into their customers' emotional needs. They've built new plants, sourced better raw materials, developed ways to tailor products for special needs, and sought more credible and knowledgeable distribution channels, such as veterinarians and specialty pet stores. It's not advertising hype—the quality is real.

What's Driving the New Luxury?

The forces propelling the democratization of luxury are various and strong, on both the supply and the demand sides. (See Exhibit 3.) Travel

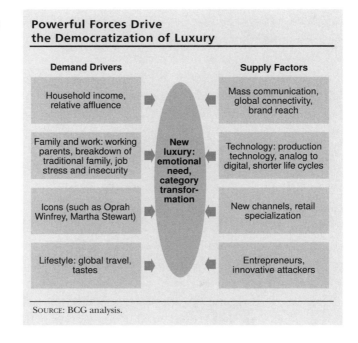

Exhibit 3 **Powerful Forces Drive the Democratization of Luxury**

Demand Drivers

- Household income, relative affluence
- Family and work: working parents, breakdown of traditional family, job stress and insecurity
- Icons (such as Oprah Winfrey, Martha Stewart)
- Lifestyle: global travel, tastes

New luxury: emotional need, category transformation

Supply Factors

- Mass communication, global connectivity, brand reach
- Technology: production technology, analog to digital, shorter life cycles
- New channels, retail specialization
- Entrepreneurs, innovative attackers

SOURCE: BCG analysis.

has created more sophisticated global tastes; technology has made possible higher quality at lower costs (78 percent of new cars have cruise control); and real income has increased considerably. Some 25 million U.S. households now earn more than $75,000 a year, and they control roughly 77 percent of the country's discretionary spending. Sixty percent of all women work outside the home, contributing almost one-third of household income; and both parents in more than half of two-parent families work.

Today's families have more disposable income, but they lack discretionary time. They feel stressed, insecure, and anxious. The typical U.S. family is working harder now than ever before—seven more hours per week per household than ten years ago. Consumers seek comforts and small pleasures that can provide an emotional salve in their hectic lives.

Working women, in particular, have to deal with the pressures of a career while maintaining the same domestic standards that their nonworking mothers did. Living well isn't only about revenge; it's also about taking care of yourself and finding some measure of emotional fulfillment. Martha Stewart and Oprah Winfrey have become enormously successful as product branders *and* role models by speaking to the emotional desires underpinning the new luxury, such as living well and in good taste, feeling inspired and optimistic, and finding happiness.

Oprah has created a movement for a generation of women. She has given women around the world permission to spend and explore, and she has introduced a new vocabulary that insiders cherish. She has defined an emotional space in which self-respect, self-indulgence, and aspiration are validated. The message she spreads is that self-love isn't narcissism: you are as beautiful as you feel, and you need to invest in yourself. With Oprah's permission, consumers can spend more for quality, raise the level of their taste, and splurge on special items.

A New Set of Rules for the New Luxury

The new luxury has shattered conventional beliefs in nearly all aspects of marketing and branding, including price ceilings, price ranges, brand extendibility, consumer sophistication, market stability, and the time it takes luxury to cascade to the middle market. Here are seven new rules for transforming your category or brand:

1. Don't underestimate the consumer. Consumers will trade up to higher levels of quality, taste, and aspiration if doing so brings them emotional and rational benefits. You have to design knowing that consumers know more than you think they do. They will reward honesty, authenticity, and integrity at the core. Robert Mondavi and Kendall Jackson discovered this rule years ago in the wine category when they challenged the long-held assumption that the U.S. palate was unsophisticated and undiscerning. The wine revolution in California, Australia, and elsewhere is still unfolding, but Americans' consumption of wine is very different today from what it was five years ago. From 1995 to 2000, wine sales grew 9 percent per year, compared with virtually flat sales for the prior decade. Consumers also traded up: prices rose three times the historical average as the mix shifted from blush and jug wines to better varietals and table wines. The trend continued in 2001: jug wine sales declined 4 percent; the under $7 segment fell 2 percent; the $7-to-$10 segment rose 6 percent; and the over $10 segment grew more than 15 percent.

2. Strive to move off the demand curve, not along it. The old rule that price and volume are inversely related does not usually hold when a category is transformed by the new luxury. Between exclusive superpremium and traditional mass market lies a rich opportunity to be tapped. With a bold vision, you can price up, spend back, and reap disproportionate profits. Starbucks did it by bringing the romance of the Italian coffee experience to mainstream USA. Victoria's Secret did it by bringing better products, a superior store experience, and great marketing to the U.S. market. Bath & Body Works created a whole new segment of daily luxuries in personal care. The "masstige" segment (premium products with mass appeal and volume) is 20 to 40 percent of many personal-care categories and growing at twice the industry average.

Sub-Zero shattered the conventional wisdom that there was no substantial household-appliance market above the $1,000 price point. Now General Electric, Maytag, and Whirlpool are struggling to meet demand for their premium lines, while Sub-Zero, with its acquisition of Wolf, is intent on doing it again in cooktops.

3. Create a technical-functional-emotional benefits ladder. Moving off the demand curve requires a breakthrough set of interrelated benefits that are both rational and emotional. To find a powerful emotional positioning, new-luxury innovators must understand the consumer's behavior, psychological map, "secret needs," and unspoken (sometimes latent) desires. They must also offer distinctive functional advantages that are specifically tied to the targeted emotions, as well as a technical platform that lends credibility and authenticity to the functional claims. Authority and expertise are critical.

If a luxury strategy is well executed, consumers will quickly "ladder" from technical to functional to emotional benefits, responding so powerfully that they will break through traditional price barriers with higher levels of demand. Pet lovers buy gourmet pet food because it is technically superior (it has added nutrients and organic ingredients), functionally reliable (experts attest to its health values), and emotionally satisfying (they are taking care of a "family member"). One word of caution: most traditional market research will miss the emotional underpinnings of new-luxury success, and conventional product testing will just as often undermine the linkages between the emotional, functional, and technical benefit layers. To generate insight, innovative players typically spend more time in the market and conduct one-on-one interviews with their core customers—in their homes, at retail sites, in their domains.

4. Escalate innovation, elevate quality, and deliver a flawless experience. The middle market is rich in opportunity, but it is also unstable. Consumers trade down as well as up. Technical and functional advantages are increasingly short-lived. The quality bar is rising at all price points. Luxury benefits are quickly cascading down-market. Nearly 80 percent of all cars have standard features that were exclusively luxury features only a few years ago. A well-established brand can't maintain an emotional position for long if the technical and functional benefits become undifferentiated. Winners in new-luxury markets aggressively up the ante on innovation and quality, and render their own products obsolete before a new competitor does it for them. What's more, their view of quality extends well beyond the product to all customer touch points: marketing, selling, service, visual merchandising, and the retail environment. They fund and treasure meaningful connections with their brand apostles and transform the experience, not just the product.

5. Stretch the brand over a broader price range with increasingly precise segmentation. The new luxury offers new ways to think about pricing and subsegmentation. Whereas a traditional competitor's highest price may be three to four times its lowest, new-luxury players often have a fivefold-to-tenfold difference between their highest and lowest price points. They take the brand up-market for aspirational appeal and extend it down-market to make it more accessible and competitive. Defending and building your market position require stretching outward from the core.

Mercedes-Benz and BMW, in an effort to combat Lexus, not only revamped their product lines; they also reconfigured their pricing and sub-segmentation strategies. In 1980, 70 percent of Mercedes' sales came from its midprice product line, 21 percent from new entry-price points, and 9 percent from the high end. Today the midprice cars represent 45 percent of sales, with 28 percent at the low end, 21 percent at the high end, and 6 percent in a new superpremium segment. BMW followed a similar pattern. Both brands have become simultaneously more accessible and aspirational, with a top price that approaches ten times the lowest. In last year's down market, BMW's unit sales grew 13 percent and average unit price actually rose slightly. The Martha Stewart brand, which stands for good taste and the best possible quality for the money, also has a tenfold price range that extends from Kmart to Martha by Mail. Mondavi does the same thing in the wine category, ranging from Woodbridge to Private Reserve and Opus One.

6. Create and own brand apostles. Heavy users drive volume and spread the word. A small percentage of category consumers contribute the dominant share of value. In categories with frequent repeat purchases, the top 10 percent of customers typically generate up to half of category sales and profits. That concentration allows for a different kind of launch model, entailing carefully managed initial sales, frequent feedback from first purchasers, unconventional marketing, and word-of-mouth recommendations. Red Bull, a premium-priced "energy" drink, has built a $100 million business without having to advertise by focusing on the social environments of its core customers: health clubs, bars, and hip hangouts. An intense focus on the core customer will also yield next-generation ideas and early signs of a shifting market.

7. Attack your category as if you were an outsider. Since outsiders have generated the majority of disruptive innovations, incumbents must find a way to break the pattern and create an outside-in approach to the evolution of their categories. Rules of thumb and everyday customer compromises are treasure maps for finding opportunity. Innovators must also look beyond their own categories for the trends and patterns that will generate the next big breakthrough. Sources of inspiration might include upmarket products or services, innovations from Europe or Asia, analogues from other categories, and advice from experts and professionals. When the makers of Freschetta Pizza, for example, sought to overtake Kraft's DiGiorno in the premium-frozen-pizza segment, they assembled a panel of five gourmet chefs from the best restaurants in the United States. The chefs, in turn, worked closely with some of the best cooking schools in Italy to develop a superior sauce and crust.

Leadership: A Call to Action

The providers of new luxury target and fill real needs that are emotional—even spiritual—as well as economic and practical. Consumers yearn to feel special. They need testaments to their self-worth and antidotes to their stresses. The movement is unstoppable, considering our times; and it is both an evolution with definable roots and drivers, and a revolution that is provoking rapid change in unexpected areas. For established competitors, it can be an opportunity or a threat. Meeting that challenge will require a new frame of reference and a different kind of leadership: more imagination and less dogma, more courage and less convention, more creativity and less incrementalism. The democratization of luxury gives imaginative leaders a new way to think about growth, profitability, and the art of fulfilling dreams.

This article was first published in April 2002.

Follow Your Dreams: An Interview with Walter Gunz, Founder of Media Markt

Alexander Lintner

Whenever businesspeople get together at conferences or in the board-room, it's not uncommon to come across such sentiments as, "How you treat your associates is as important as how you treat your balance sheet" or "Success is as much about having fun as it is about winning." But how many hard-nosed business managers really believe those words, let alone act on them?

In an environment of cutthroat competition and unrelenting shareholder pressure, staying true to your heart while leading with your head isn't always easy or, perhaps, even wise. Yet one very successful executive has done just that over a long and triumphant career. Walter Gunz—founder of Media Markt, Europe's largest retailer of consumer electronics—believes that treating people with respect and decency is, in fact, cru-

Walter Gunz

cial to long-lasting success. Allowing associates to dream, act on their intu-itions, and take control of their destiny is the key to good retailing; control from above, hierarchical organizations, and micromanagement, by contrast, prevent people from achieving their full potential.

Born in Munich in 1946, Gunz studied philosophy and economics before joining Karstadt Warenhaus, Europe's largest department-store chain, where he rose to become head of the consumer electronics department in the Munich store. He left Karstadt in 1979 and, shortly thereafter, founded Media Markt in Munich with a shoestring staff and only DM 20,000. Ten years later, the company became part of the Metro Group, the world's fourth-largest retailer. When Gunz sold his remaining shares in Media Markt to the Metro Group some 21 years after its founding, the chain had 300 outlets in 11 countries, 18,000 employees, annual sales of $7 billion, and profits of $300 million. Today Media Markt—which could be compared to Best Buy in the United States—is still one of the fastest-growing retailers in Europe, as well as one of the most profitable players in the retail electronics sector.

Gunz's accomplishment isn't just a matter of luck or talent. His deep concern for his employees, suppliers, and customers is, in fact, at the heart of his achievement. In view of today's business uncertainties and global tensions, we thought this might be a good time to talk with Gunz. Alexander Lintner, a vice president in the Munich office of The Boston Consulting Group and head of the firm's Retail practice in Europe, spoke with Gunz about his experience in the retail sector and his conviction that all employees should find joy in their work.

You've had a great deal of success in your life, and you've met a lot of successful people. What qualities do you believe are most important for making it to the top?

Contrary to what many people seem to think, you don't get there by behaving like a jerk. Yet the pursuit of success can sometimes cause people to act like jerks. Many senior executives succumb to the hubris of power once they feel they've outplayed their competition. They start taking themselves too seriously and lose their capacity to empathize with the people around them. That's why success can sometimes be harmful. But truly great leaders get through this stage. The biggest challenge for those who have made it to the top—a challenge that goes hand in hand with remaining there—is to stay true to the person you were before you became successful.

Can you tell us how Media Markt was born?

In the 1960s, after I finished university, I started working at the Karstadt department store. Karstadt was doing very well back then, and its buyers were among the most respected in the industry. Much to my surprise, I did pretty well there, too. Karstadt was a very centralized, hierarchical place, and I tended to make my own decisions and bent a number of company rules. Eventually, I had to leave, because I wouldn't do things their way.

I was sure that I had ruined my career by quitting. It took me a couple of months before I figured out what to do next. One night I had dinner with some people who had worked directly under me at Karstadt. They were as frustrated with their jobs as I had been and wanted to come work for me. But what would we do? In trying to answer that question, it occurred to me that the only thing I could do really well was sell, and the only products I knew anything about were electronics. So we decided to go into the electronics business together.

Over the next few months, my team of 11 ex-Karstadt employees and I presented our plan for an electronics superstore to several industry suppliers that I had gotten to know in my Karstadt days. Although there were already quite a few electronics specialty stores around, the suppliers promised to deliver their products—if we paid on time. Then I heard that the entrepreneur Erich Kellerhals was looking for a company to invest in. I didn't have much of a company yet—just DM 20,000 borrowed from my mother and a handful of enthusiastic people—but I thought it might be enough to attract Erich, and it was. What I didn't know at the time was that several of Erich's stores were doing poorly. Yet despite that—and the fact that we lacked the necessary finances—Erich, his partner Leopold Stiefel, and I opened the first Media Markt in Munich.

I was very nervous the night before the opening. All I could think of was that we had to sell DM 200,000 worth of goods on the first day to get out of the red. I had dreams of doing more than that, of course, but I suddenly realized that we could just as easily do considerably less. And if that happened, we'd be broke. Fortune smiled on us, however: we turned over DM 324,000 the first day. That wasn't a bad figure for a store at that time.

You still had a long way to go to get to where you are today. To what do you attribute Media Markt's eventual success?

It all depends on how you measure success. Have you achieved it when sales go up 20 percent, or does it take 40 percent? The numbers, of course, are relative. Media Markt's success was a combination of many things, but at the beginning it had everything to do with the people. We were a small crew, but we had a big vision. Our dream was to run a company in which everyone could find joy in his or her work. We all remembered our time at Karstadt—our fear of the supervisors and the awkwardness of our interactions with them. None of us wanted to experience that again. We discovered that if you treated people decently, work could be fun.

Of course, external factors also contributed to our success. But our people were key, and I think that's true for most businesses. I'm not necessarily advocating bonuses or profit sharing for everyone, but we turned our store managers into true partners by giving them a percentage of the store for which they were responsible. In doing so, we ensured that the many decisions that are best made on-site, such as purchasing, would be good decisions because the managers had an incentive to make sure they were good. We also decentralized pricing: each store manager decided which price was most appropriate in his or her competitive environment.

Ten years after we began our glorious journey, we looked into the future and decided we were too small. So we sold a major part of our company to the Metro Group and became part of a large corporation—with all the inherent advantages and disadvantages that poses for a company. However, thanks to carefully written contracts, we were able to prevent our parent company and fellow subsidiaries from gaining more influence than would have been healthy for us. At the same time, we were protected from other large foreign companies in the same sector entering the market. We really had the best of both worlds. It wasn't easy, of course, but we managed it.

We hear a lot about "emotional leadership" these days. What does that mean to you, if anything?

It's a trendy phrase, but I've never understood exactly what people mean by it. For me, I guess, it has something to do with honesty in communication: being as straight with people as you can. You know, supervisors don't always tell the truth in employee appraisals. Employees may not know exactly what their boss is holding back. But I think most of them sense it when something is not being said, and of course that makes them uneasy. We're all guilty of being less than genuine at certain times in our lives, but I believe it is particularly important in business to treat others as you would want to be treated.

But can you be entirely open with everyone in business? What about suppliers?

I've always wanted to view our suppliers as partners, but I think it's in the nature of most businesses to become less open as they become more successful. The hubris of power begins when you think you have to squeeze as much as possible out of your suppliers and partners. Yet it doesn't automatically follow that you have to disregard the interests of others to get the best for yourself. In a true partnership, you want everyone to come out ahead. If you get a good deal, the other party should get one as well. And we have proof that it works: to this day, the terms that we achieve at Media Markt are better than the terms that our parent, the Metro Group, achieves, although Metro is larger. That's because Metro always tries to pressure its suppliers.

Treating people with fairness and respect is what we all strive for in business as well as in life. After all, we spend most of our lives at work, and if we don't find peace of mind there, where will we find it?

How do you balance being a "good guy" with the profit motive and your commitment to your shareholders to create value?

When the Berlin Wall fell and East and West Germany came together, I was asked to speak before a group of former directors of major state-run enterprises. Everyone was fixated on the profits and luxuries that supposedly would soon follow. I wanted to offer them an alternative picture because I knew that establishing a market economy was going to be harder than people thought. So I told a Zen Buddhist story about a wise archer who never aims at the target but nevertheless hits the bull's-eye every time. His secret is that he understands the importance of not being overly fixated on the goal. Every one of us has the power to hit the target. But there's a big difference between trying hard to hit it and believing you can hit it. As soon as I want something badly and feel I must have it, I tense up inside, and it becomes more difficult to use the natural talents I might have to reach my goal. But if I have faith and believe in my success, it's more likely that I will actually achieve it.

I think that is a good philosophy for doing business. If we concentrate on profits to the exclusion of everything else, they won't materialize. I firmly believe that profits come only as a consequence of really caring about the process: outperforming your competitors in customer satisfaction, creating a good place to work, offering quality merchandise. You can have profits, even large profits, and you're allowed to enjoy them. But you can't strive for profit for profit's sake—you'd lose your ability to relax and would eventually overshoot the target.

How do you keep generating fresh ideas in a large, successful company?

We are constantly adapting our goals as new circumstances arise. We don't hold on to tradition for tradition's sake—everything is up for grabs. We try to encourage change, and we don't give up if success isn't immediate. Not all ideas are necessarily good ones, but at Media Markt you can make a mistake without being punished. Of course, we don't want the staff to keep making the same mistakes, so we've figured out a kind of self-teaching system that allows people to learn from their blunders without feeling too bad about them. You can't have fun if you're worried about screwing up, and you're successful only as long as you feel your work is fun.

You talk a lot about having fun. What exactly do you mean by that?

Work should be like a good, competitive game. Too much seriousness leads to an overblown sense of importance, which in turn produces an enormous amount of stress when the numbers aren't as high as you think they should be. You become afraid to take risks and are always looking for someone else to blame. That's no fun.

You've given us an idea of what success looks like to you. What about failure? Why do businesses fail?

Failures in business arise from the same causes as failures in life: greed for money, power, and success. The fear of failure is what hampers creativity. Fear is the greatest destroyer of energy. Look at how threatened subordinates are made to feel at many companies—it's no surprise that those companies suffer from a lack of innovative ideas.

Lack of trust is another factor in failure. Organizations become excessively bureaucratic when people don't trust one another. That's especially true for larger companies, in which the need for control can become an obsession. When that happens, it threatens the whole business because these organizations suffer when entrepreneurial activity is stymied.

Ironically, most companies make their mistakes when they are at the peak of their power. Failure comes not from the outside but from within. Like the Romans before the fall of their empire, organizations begin to take their success for granted and then are surprised when someone takes it away from them.

You believe that strong brands are important. How do you create a great brand?

Consider a Van Gogh painting. Why is it valued at $30 million today when the artist received barely the price of a dinner for painting it? The reason, I feel, is that Van Gogh's paintings represent something we desperately need in our cultural wasteland. Today, instead of great composers, painters, and architects, we have technicians who develop one laptop after another or who decode DNA. Brands have become a substitute for culture. As real culture disappears, brands become more significant. That's why they are now so extraordinarily important: we define ourselves with them. Therefore, brands must be genuine to satisfy our needs. They must stand for what consumers *need* them to stand for, as well as for what the company *wants* them to stand for.

Today even successful brands are under pressure from shareholders to produce short-term profits. How does that affect managing a brand?

The stock market has forced managers to become obsessed about their stock price, day in and day out, to the detriment of long-term business goals. The speculator frenzy has gone so far that every soccer club is becoming a joint-stock corporation. Interestingly, the Islamic religion forbids paying interest on money because Muslims believe that value can be created only through real work. Please don't misunderstand me: I am a firm believer in capitalism, and I'm thoroughly convinced that its free and open capital markets are superior to other systems. Nevertheless, there is merit in the idea that real value in both our personal and business lives can be achieved only through *producing* something of real value.

If you could sum up your philosophy of management in a few words, what would it be?

We have more freedom than we think. Through our words, our actions, even our dreams, we can accomplish truly great things. In my business dealings, I find it useful to remember the words of Antoine de Saint-Exupéry: "It is only with the heart that one can see rightly; what is essential is invisible to the eye." In other words, happiness and success will be ours only if we remain authentic and grateful. Therefore, the happiness and satisfaction of our clients, employees, and business associates must always be our deepest concern.

This article was first published in May 2002.

Recovering the Pricing Opportunity

Ulrika Dellby and Henry M. Vogel

Pricing is an extremely powerful value driver for most consumer and retail companies. Thanks to the availability of specific data on SKUs, stores, and consumers, we are entering a new era in pricing science. By carefully testing their data in controlled experiments, managers can raise or lower prices with virtually no risk. The payoff will come when they discover true demand elasticity and unleash new sources of profitable growth.

Most companies, however, fail to capture all of the opportunities for generating growth, profit, and competitive advantage through pricing. What's more, many companies do an especially poor job of managing pricing as they come out of an economic downturn. Few plan for recovery or pull the right pricing levers at the right time. They aren't prepared to price—either up or down—in response to changing market conditions or competitive dynamics. Yet such changes offer an opportunity for action that companies cannot afford to miss.

In many instances, managers base pricing decisions on gut instinct and incomplete or inaccurate information. If you ask most managers how they price, you often get a simplistic response—for instance, "to meet our plan"—or a complicated one that fails to be based on discipline, competitive advantage, or creativity. Managers often cling to their old belief, formed during previous downturns, that they can't raise prices; and they give up that belief only after the recovery is well under way and opportunities have passed them by.

Companies that prepare pricing strategies for specific business-cycle scenarios and employ the appropriate pricing levers stand to reap significant rewards in the form of profits and competitive advantage. Of course, the potential rewards vary by company and product. They depend not only on the cost structures, competitive dynamics, and demand elasticities of individual businesses or categories but also on the timing and shape of the recovery in the specific sector or region.

Even small price increases can have a considerable impact on the bottom line, and there are more ways to raise or lower prices than many consumer companies realize. The key to gaining ground—even in tougher times—is to know exactly which levers to pull every step along the way and to be prepared to pull them quickly. In other words, you should implement the pricing strategies most appropriate for the competitive dynamic, your strategic objectives, and each point in the business cycle.

In our experience, three basic elements are required in order to manage pricing effectively in a recovery:

1. An understanding of the pricing patterns in your business

2. A knowledge of which pricing levers to pull

3. An organization that can execute your strategy boldly and aggressively

Understand the Pricing Patterns in Your Business

Most companies recognize the specific factors in their business or category that drive pricing power and performance—factors such as their product's economics or their competitors' reactions to pricing moves. However, few companies fully appreciate the broader macroeconomic factors that affect pricing. Understanding the pricing patterns in your sector or category in specific types of recoveries in the past is a good starting point.

We reviewed all the downturns in the United States since the late 1940s that were classified as recessions by the National Bureau of Economic Research. In our review, we observed four basic categories of recession-and-recovery, one of which occurred several times: one V Curve, five Slow Builds, one period of Stagflation, and one Double Dip. That perspective also revealed clear inflation patterns in each type of recovery. The V-Curve recovery and the period of Stagflation had the highest general rates of consumer price inflation, whereas inflation was curbed in the various Slow

Builds and, to a lesser degree, in the second recovery of the Double Dip. (See Exhibit 1.)

Even more important, however, are the shape of the recovery and the pricing implications in your specific sector. For each sector, it is important to ascertain

- the nature of your specific business cycle

- your pricing patterns and how they relate to inventories, consumer loyalty and switching behavior, and other critical factors that affect pricing

- how changes in demand elasticity, cost structures, and competitive dynamics might affect those pricing patterns and relationships

- whether any competitors have significantly changed their pricing strategies or introduced new, innovative pricing tactics, as they often do during times of economic turbulence

Not surprisingly, there is a lot of variation in pricing and inflation across consumer sectors. Exhibit 2 illustrates the change in the consumer price index (CPI) for individual sectors during the recessions we studied.

The recession that appears to be ending in the United States posted one of the sharpest drops in CPI across most sectors. Although consumer spending remained relatively robust, buyers were driven largely by steep price discounts and reductions. Such deflation suggests a pent-up corporate demand for pricing actions that, given even a modest recovery, should help support higher prices in many sectors.

Know Which Pricing Levers to Pull

Be prepared to capture your pricing opportunity. Although no one can predict the exact shape and timing of the recovery—and it can vary quite significantly by sector—the current one appears to be shaping up as a V Curve or a relatively fast Slow Build. However, another external shock could lead to a Double Dip. Therefore, you should design pricing strategies for several scenarios based on your best estimate of how the recovery will affect the demand elasticities, cost structures, and competitive dynamics of your particular sector and business.

Exhibit 1

Pricing out of Recessions Differs by Type of Recovery

Different Levels, Direction, and Timing of Price Increases

V Curve: Steep Price Increases

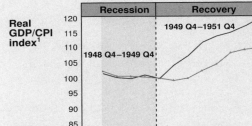

Real GDP/CPI index[1]

	Recession	Recovery

1948 Q4–1949 Q4

1949 Q4–1951 Q4

Quarters pre and post recession

CAGR (%)[2]

Recovery
GDP   9.2
CPI   5.5

Recession
GDP −1.6
CPI −2.2

Stagflation: Steepest Increases (external oil shock)

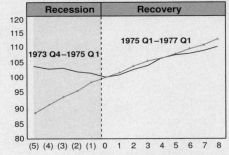

Real GDP/CPI index

	Recession	Recovery

1973 Q4–1975 Q1

1975 Q1–1977 Q1

Quarters pre and post recession

CAGR (%)

Recovery
GDP   4.9
CPI   6.1

Recession
GDP −2.7
CPI 10.6

―――― GDP   ―●― CPI   Shading represents recession periods as defined by the NBER

SOURCES: National Bureau of Economic Research (NBER); Bureau of Labor Statistics; Bureau of Economic Analysis; BCG analysis.

[1]Real GDP and CPI were indexed to 100 at the ending quarter of a recession and the beginning quarter of a recovery.
[2]Compounded annual growth rate was calculated from quarter 0 to quarter 8 for recoveries and in the shaded quarters for recessions.
[3]Of the five Slow Build recoveries since the late 1940s, we selected 1957 as a representative example.

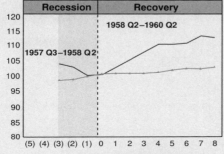

Slow Build: Flat to Moderate Increases[3]

Real GDP/CPI index

Recession | Recovery

1958 Q2–1960 Q2

1957 Q3–1958 Q2

(5) (4) (3) (2) (1) 0 1 2 3 4 5 6 7 8

Quarters pre and post recession

CAGR (%)
Recovery
GDP 5.7
CPI 1.1

Recession
GDP −4.2
CPI 2.8

Double Dip: Volatile Pricing as Inflation Is Curbed

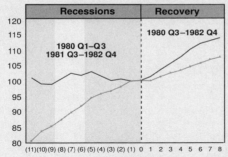

Real GDP/CPI index

Recessions | Recovery

1980 Q3–1982 Q4

1980 Q1–Q3
1981 Q3–1982 Q4

(11)(10)(9) (8) (7) (6) (5) (4) (3) (2) (1) 0 1 2 3 4 5 6 7 8

Quarters pre and post recession

CAGR (%)
Recovery
First Second
GDP 0.6 6.6
CPI 8.3 3.7
Recession
First Second
GDP −4.3 −2.2
CPI 11.5 4.8

Exhibit 2

Deflationary CPI Trends Have Been Steeper in the Most Recent Recession Than They Were in the Past 50 Years

Pent-Up Demand for Pricing Action in Most Sectors

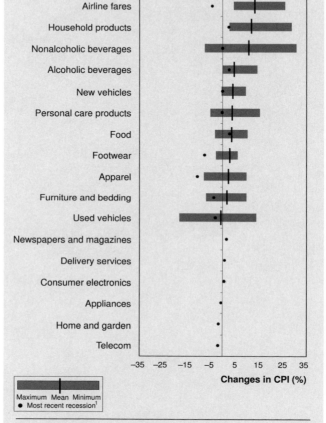

SOURCES: Bureau of Labor Statistics; BCG analysis.

NOTE: Data were calculated by industry for every recession since 1947 (excluding the most recent one), with the exceptions of alcoholic beverages and used vehicles (which reflect recessions since 1953) and household products and airline fares (recessions since 1963). For industries without historical data, only the most recent recession is shown.
[1]Calculated from March 2001 to January 2002.

Understanding the consumer value equation and demand elasticity for your categories is an important foundation for any good pricing strategy; it is especially important during inflection points in the business cycle. Unfortunately, many consumer companies don't have sufficient information on (or insight about) the actual demand elasticity of their products and services.

For example, we recently calculated demand elasticities and tested new pricing options for a number of clients. Demand elasticity in quick-service restaurants, it turns out, is high, offering an opportunity for clients that reduce prices and sell new value to consumers to dramatically improve their perceived value, volume, profit, and share. But in other businesses, such as food ingredients, demand elasticity is very low. If prices are reduced, demand and volume remain unchanged but the manufacturer's profits go down. It is crucial to know the elasticity of every item by channel, geographic location, and target customer.

One framework we use to assist in the optimization of pricing strategies plots the average product-contribution margin (the incremental profit generated from selling one more unit) against the resulting breakeven elasticity for a variety of consumer sectors. (See Exhibit 3.) By *breakeven elasticity*,

Exhibit 3   **Pricing Potential Varies Depending on Cost Structure and Product Demand Elasticity**

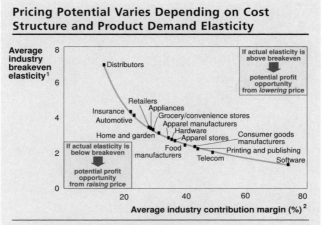

SOURCES: Compustat data; BCG analysis.
[1]*Breakeven elasticity* is defined as the point at which the operating profit of an average company in the industry remains unchanged in response to a change in price.
[2]Based on the weighted average cost structure of publicly traded companies in the industry.

we mean the point where the change in volume resulting from a change in price will have no impact on the operating profit of an average company in the industry. This elasticity is measured as the percentage volume decline given a 1 percent change in price.

All else being equal, if the *actual* demand elasticity for your sector's product or service is below the breakeven line, raising the price will drive higher profits, even after the drop-off in volume resulting from the price increase. By contrast, if the actual elasticity is above the breakeven line, lower prices will drive sufficiently higher demand to increase overall net profits.

Understanding this dynamic and the optimal price point that generates the maximum amount of profit is a key strategic advantage. We call this *precision pricing*, and it is driven by the *pricing profit parabola*. Moving to your optimal parabola price generates the greatest amount of profits, whereas understanding your competitors' profit parabolas will help identify their weaknesses and your relative advantages.

Take the example of a leading consumer packaged-goods (CPG) company. It was facing an aggressive competitor that focused on price-oriented retailers, such as discount mass merchandisers and club stores. (See Exhibit 4.) Although the CPG company sold high-margin, highly elastic products and often used promotions to drive volume and profit, it didn't understand the true product-demand elasticities by channel. In fact, its prices were above the optimal point on the profit parabola in many price-oriented stores. Its competitor, however, had managed to persuade these retailers to charge prices below the optimal point, even though it didn't support the discounts. Discounting in this channel became especially important during the downturn.

Once the CPG company understood this dynamic, it changed course and de-averaged its pricing strategy by channel and account. It lowered prices and began to promote its products more aggressively in mass and club stores. What's more, the facts that it had gathered about the pricing dynamic helped it persuade the retailers to adjust the price on the competitor's products. As a result, the company and its retail partners achieved significant growth in volume, share, *and* profits.

This example highlights another important point. Actual demand elasticities often fluctuate with changes in the broader economic environment, and that fluctuation varies by channel. In general, consumers—individuals

Exhibit 4   **Precision Pricing Maximizes Returns and Advantage**

Example: Leading Manufacturer of Consumer Packaged Goods

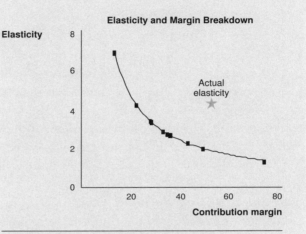

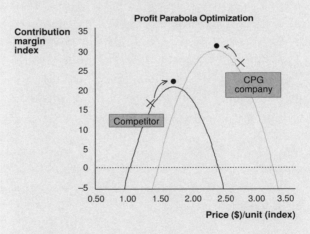

SOURCE: BCG analysis.

and businesses—become more sensitive to price during economic down-turns. Household purses and corporate profits are pinched, and spending is delayed, because of the uncertainty. As consumers become more optimistic and corporate coffers begin to fill during recoveries, demand elasticities tend to become less acute.

A comparison of year-over-year growth in same-store sales for different retailers demonstrates this point. (See Exhibit 5.) Whereas discount and off-price stores have been able to increase their same-store sales during the down-turn, higher-priced stores—department stores, traditional supermarkets, and specialty retailers—have seen a significant decline in sales, even after dramatic price reductions.

Understanding whether and how consumers will change their behavior again during the nascent stages of the recovery is essential. Such an under-standing will require you to know how your sector or industry will respond to the emerging recovery.

Pricing into a V-Curve Recovery. Companies in sectors that are already rebounding faster than the overall economy, and where elasticity is more lim-ited, should plan more aggressive price increases. Take the extreme case of cable and satellite TV providers. Their sector benefited during the recent downturn from relatively robust consumer spending in general and from healthy spending on "affordable luxuries" in particular, including the enter-tainment services they provide. They also enjoy comparatively significant pric-ing power. A number of these players have taken rather aggressive and transparent pricing actions:

- Directv, the leading satellite-TV player in some markets, recently eliminated a low-priced programming bundle for new subscribers and raised by 10 percent the price for existing customers who chose to retain those programs

- Comcast, another cable giant, has been hiking prices throughout the recession and has raised them by 15 percent or more in some markets

Pricing Strategies for a Slow Build. If your sector is facing a slower recovery or if the strength of the rebound is still unclear, be prepared to manage pricing with hidden or less visible levers that can be more easily tai-

Exhibit 5

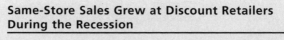

Same-Store Sales Grew at Discount Retailers During the Recession

But They Declined at Higher-Priced Traditional Retailers

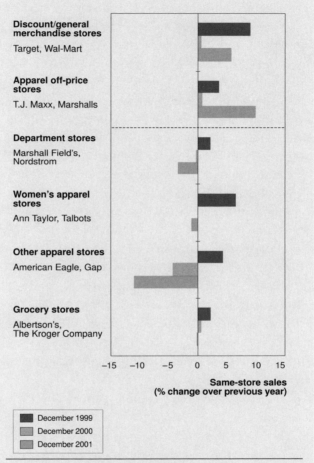

SOURCES: Prudential Securities; BCG analysis.

NOTE: Data are available quarterly for grocery stores; therefore, the bars compare the fourth quarters of 1999 and 1998, 2000 and 1999, and 2001 and 2000. Each sector comprises many companies. The above stores were selected as representative examples.

lored for individual customer segments or channels. Less visible price increases or cuts might include surcharges, temporary off-invoice discounts or volume-building pricing programs, and relaxed terms or extended credit. Adjusting the frequency, type, and depth of a promotion—as well as channel, product, or geographic focus—to optimize price realization are some of the most important price levers available to consumer and retail companies.

Compared with more *transparent* price mechanisms (such as changes in list prices), less visible and more temporary discounts or increases provide companies with greater flexibility and leverage to manage the price-volume tradeoff. Because hidden price increases are less visible to consumers, they can have a more limited impact on volume. In addition, temporary price reductions set less of a precedent and are easier to change if and when a more robust rebound occurs. Such discounts can provide a way to share the pain with consumers in the short term, without destroying your long-term price point and brand equity. If and when the V Curve materializes, then bolder, more transparent increases can still be implemented.

Consider airlines, one of the industries hardest hit by the September 11 attacks and their aftermath. Although the dramatic falloff in both corporate and leisure traffic may have stabilized, renewed growth is by no means certain. This is also an industry with very high overall demand elasticity, especially in the leisure travel segment. Nonetheless, airlines have managed to enact a series of hidden price increases—including security, passenger-facility, and fuel surcharges—along with more segmented corporate discounts. In addition, several travel agencies have begun charging for their services.

Preparing for a Potential Double Dip. Recovery from this recession is not yet certain. War, terror, oil price increases, or other external forces could derail the recovery and throw the world into a Double Dip recession. In that case, aggressive action to lower prices might be in order. The zero-percent-financing strategy that General Motors implemented after the September 11 attacks is a good example of the kind of responsive action that companies should prepare. The initiative, which GM artfully packaged as a patriotic effort, was bold, decisive, and clearly communicated. It captured consumers' imaginations and caught competitors off guard. Just as important, the program was strategically designed to leverage GM's strengths and exploit its competitors' weaknesses. Those strengths include the company's

- lower borrowing costs, which meant the program cost GM less than it would have cost Ford and DaimlerChrysler

- lower exposure to leases, which meant that the resulting lower resale value of cars coming off leases would hurt GM less

- richer pipeline of new products, which put GM in a stronger position to weather the storm if the promotion stole from future industry sales

By being prepared, GM was able to act quickly and capture the first mover's advantage. That speed helped the automaker define the playing field and set the pricing terms to its advantage.

Organize to Execute Boldly and Aggressively

One major problem that many companies—especially consumer companies—face is that they are not organized to price effectively. Consequently, they often miss opportunities or act too late to capture them. Although many people *touch* pricing, few people actually *own* it in most companies. Pricing decisions, expertise, and information are often fragmented and diffused across regions, business units, and functions. Good metrics and processes to monitor pricing opportunities or threats and to measure performance are lacking, making it difficult to understand the true impact of pricing actions. Moreover, incentives are often misaligned, creating disconnects between a company's overall business strategy and its pricing tactics and performance. All this helps to explain why so many companies are not prepared to anticipate or take appropriate pricing action as recoveries unfold.

Upgrading pricing into a world-class capability can be a significant challenge, given the numerous parts of the organization involved in making and implementing pricing decisions. Marketing departments often set list or gross prices, but the sales department then determines net prices by setting the frequency, type, and depth of promotions, as well as other volume discounts or rebate programs. In addition, many other decisions, such as payment terms, minimum-order sizes, or freight brackets—often not considered in the pricing equation—are determined by the finance or operations department and are, in effect, services provided at a set or discounted price. Finally, it is often the customer service representative at the front line who will or will not enforce pricing policies. Few companies organize for pricing success by having the right people, processes, and metrics in place to coordinate, monitor, and manage this complexity. Too often, the result is poor execution and significant price leakage.

There's no way around the fact that pricing is complex—too complex for quick fixes. However, one thing is clear: the current economic environment demands immediate action. One valuable step that companies can take now is to mobilize a SWAT team of senior managers to plan the pricing scenarios. These managers would monitor the leading economic indicators for their industry, identify the type of recovery as it emerges, and lead the efforts to execute pricing strategies.

Pricing for Growth, Profit, and Advantage

Although most companies have focused on cost reduction during the economic slowdown, turning to precision pricing now can be a much more powerful way to drive growth and improve profits, market share, and competitive position.

The following five questions can help you determine if you are prepared to capture the pricing opportunity:

- Have you established a pricing SWAT team to own pricing and armed it with all the analytic tools for precision pricing?

- Have you determined the type of recovery that is unfolding in your sector and designed pricing strategies to optimize your profits and competitive position?

- Have you developed contingency plans and designed pricing strategies for other types of recovery, especially a Double Dip?

- Have you mapped your competitors' likely actions or reactions and your responses?

- Are you confident that several months from now you will not look back and rue the missed opportunities to reap greater profits and enhance your competitive position?

Taking the actions necessary to answer these questions with an enthusiastic *yes* will help you build a new strategic capability for managing pricing throughout the current economic cycle. It may also initiate a fundamental restructuring of your pricing capabilities to enhance your pricing prowess and generate long-term sustainable value and competitive advantage.

This article was first published in June 2002.

Winning the New-Product War

François Dalens, Jeff Gell, Carl Rutstein, and Robert Birge

Pressure to deliver top-line growth has forced many marketers to increase their spending on new-product development and to raise their launch budgets. Unfortunately, the economics of bringing new products to market have been skyrocketing, with higher raw advertising-delivery costs, increased retailer stocking and listing fees, and bigger investments necessary for R&D. Greater product variety has added complexity and cost to the production process even as consumer adoption rates have plummeted. The net result is a paradox: the stock markets demand growth, so consumer companies try harder to develop new products—but the higher spending results in lower earnings.

In research conducted with TBWA\Chiat\Day, The Boston Consulting Group documented four common problems in recent new-product launches:

- There is little in the way of a compelling consumer proposition

- The sizing of the market potential is superficial

- A tight link between the launch model and the underlying profit pool is lacking

- The processes to kill bad product ideas are ineffective

Those factors have resulted in a meager 20 percent success rate on products with launch budgets of more than $25 million.

WebVan, for example, burned nearly a billion dollars attempting to build a grocery home-delivery service. Concept testing would have shown that fewer than 5 percent of U.S. households were willing to adopt the particular home-delivery model that WebVan was counting on to capture the dominant share of their grocery purchases. World Wrestling Entertainment and NBC wasted more than $100 million trying to launch the XFL, an alternative football league. The result was mediocre football with exotic dancers as cheerleaders. The league failed after one season.

There are similar examples in almost every category of consumer goods and retail. Marketers hoping to reinvigorate their product portfolios should be saying to themselves: "I am playing a high-risk game. It's a minefield for failure. If I want to avoid cataclysmic loss, I will need a product launch model with checkpoints and hurdles. I will also need a review process that is consistent and economically grounded."

A Tougher Environment

The environment for bringing new products to market couldn't get any more daunting. The cost of television advertising is steadily mounting at the same time that commercials are becoming less effective. CPMs (costs per thousand impressions) for prime-time television have more than doubled, in real terms, over the past 25 years, while the time that consumers spend watching prime-time TV is decreasing. What's more, the major networks can no longer claim the lion's share of viewers, making it harder to reach a mass audience with one commercial. And with more channels coming into the home, consumers are being bombarded with so many messages that it is unlikely any one message will rise above the clutter.

Moreover, consumer audiences have become fragmented over the past several decades. The popular television programs of the 1950s, such as *Father Knows Best* and *The Donna Reed Show*, were mirrors—albeit idealized ones—of the vast majority of traditional families: middle-class, with working fathers and shopping mothers. Just about any new household product could be launched with one broad-based television campaign targeting moms. Sam Johnson, for example, successfully launched Glade, Raid, and Pledge to 1950s mothers during soap operas.

Now the mass market for household products includes many dual-income and single-parent families, as well as traditional moms, and it represents a spectrum of lifestyles. Given the range of interests and backgrounds among today's mass-market consumers, a single prime-time television commercial no longer has sufficient reach. It can cost three times as much as it did even in 1995 to send a message to most segments of the population. (See Exhibits 1–3.)

Exhibit 1   **Advertising Rates Have Escalated
While Reach and Depth Have Declined**

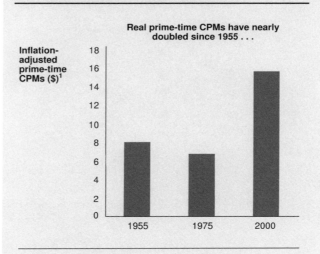

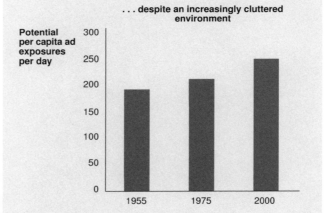

SOURCES: Media Dynamics; Nielsen's National Television Audience
Survey, 2000.
NOTE: CPMs are in 2000 dollars.
[1]Costs per thousand impressions.

Exhibit 2   **More Channels, Fewer Viewers**

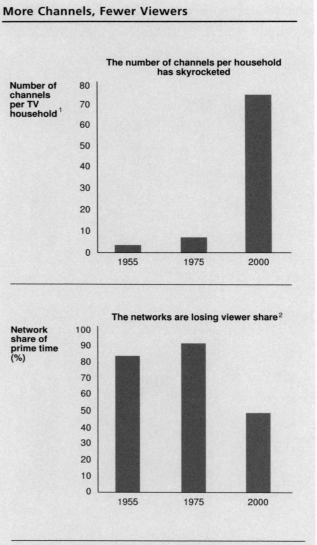

SOURCES: Media Dynamics; Nielsen's National Television Audience Survey, 2000.
[1]Data for 1955 and 1975 were approximated using 1950 and 1970 data.
[2]Includes Fox.

Exhibit 3

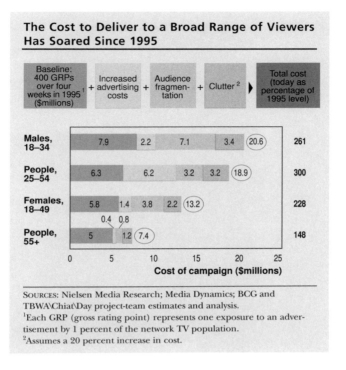

The Cost to Deliver to a Broad Range of Viewers Has Soared Since 1995

SOURCES: Nielsen Media Research; Media Dynamics; BCG and TBWA\Chiat\Day project-team estimates and analysis.
[1]Each GRP (gross rating point) represents one exposure to an advertisement by 1 percent of the network TV population.
[2]Assumes a 20 percent increase in cost.

The economics of launching new products have changed in other ways as well. The struggle for adequate market share is becoming much tougher as the balance of power shifts from suppliers to sellers. Consolidating retailers have put pressure on manufacturers to lower costs and spend more on trade at the expense of product launch advertising. And the growth in large superstores means that more shelf space is available for competitors' products as well as one's own. (See Exhibit 4.)

But the problem isn't just in the external business environment. Factors inside companies also play a huge role in making the investment in product launches much riskier. Most organizations, for example, are now rotating brand managers through different departments every few years. That means brand managers are under tremendous pressure to develop and launch a blockbuster during their relatively short time in a position. Because they aren't likely to be around for the long term, a product that might gain a following slowly over a few years isn't nearly as exciting to them as a six-month wonder. And finally, when you take into account that R&D costs have risen sharply (see Exhibit 5), an ambitious brand manager without real

Exhibit 4

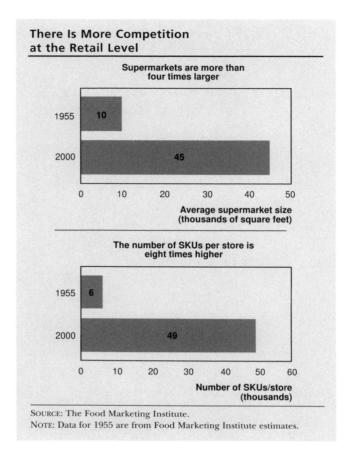

There Is More Competition at the Retail Level

Supermarkets are more than four times larger

1955 — 10
2000 — 45

Average supermarket size (thousands of square feet)

The number of SKUs per store is eight times higher

1955 — 6
2000 — 49

Number of SKUs/store (thousands)

SOURCE: The Food Marketing Institute.
NOTE: Data for 1955 are from Food Marketing Institute estimates.

accountability for products launched during his watch can squander a lot of resources.

Starting Small

According to some industry surveys, 90 percent of new-product launches attract less than 1 percent market share. A CFO of a large consumer company recently tracked its last ten launches. Each launch had cost $40 million to $60 million in media advertising alone. But only one product of the ten—an incremental improvement, as it turned out—was considered to have been worth the investment.

Across nearly every category, new-product launches have become losing propositions that deplete shareholder value and company resources. Yet many companies continue to throw good money after bad, figuring that if they spend enough, they'll eventually capture a market. It's a doomed strategy. Except for a few mass-market products, such as Gillette's Mach 3 razor—which was a true innovation directed at a broad target from a dominant position—creating a big bang with a blockbuster campaign is too costly and imprecise for today's expensive and fragmented environment. Instead, product launchers need to take better aim at targeted segments of consumers—wherever they might find them—and build on incremental successes. That way, advertising budgets won't be likely to exceed expected sales.

New Launch Models

Red Bull, a company that sells an energy drink with the same name, has managed to make this smarter approach to product launches pay off. The drink was introduced in Europe in the 1980s but only recently came to the United States. Rather than set out to capture the U.S. mass market with an expensive national advertising campaign, Red Bull began by focusing on people aged 16 to 29. The company then rolled out its campaign one region at a time and learned what worked best before going on to the next region.

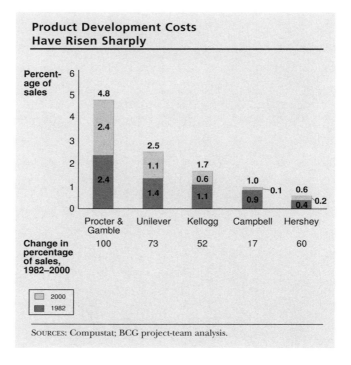

Exhibit 5

Product Development Costs Have Risen Sharply

SOURCES: Compustat; BCG project-team analysis.

One particularly successful strategy was to create a buzz about the product even before it hit the market. By offering free samples through sports clubs and bars, Red Bull generated so much interest in the drink that when it did appear in stores, it sold off the shelves. Red Bull also shopped for the hungriest distributors to keep the costs of deals low. As demand for the product grew, the company could increase its spending on promotion. By concentrating on local markets and core consumers, by building excitement for the product before placing it in stores, and by rolling it out market by market, Red Bull developed a highly successful new drink—one that eventually reached the mainstream.

As traditional advertising becomes more costly and carries less of a punch, today's brand managers have to look for other "touch points" where they can deliver their messages more effectively, at lower costs. These might include film and radio, the Internet, the telephone, live entertainment, newspapers, billboards, magazines, books, direct mail, store samplings, sponsored sporting events, music festivals, academic conferences, and, of course, "brand ambassadors"—influential people who serve as role models for other consumers. Such an approach helped Vespa create excitement about its new scooters in the United States. It hired glamorous models to ride them to popular hot spots in Los Angeles and talk about why they loved their Vespas. The company spent a minimal amount on marketing yet doubled its sales.

Or consider Chrysler's unorthodox strategy for introducing the PT Cruiser. Rather than using a nationwide media blitz, the company piqued the interest of drivers by placing the distinctive-looking new model in several rental-car fleets throughout trendsetting metropolitan Miami. People saw the car on the road and wanted to know more about it. Television news stations began to pick up on the interest, and suddenly Chrysler had free advertising. Chrysler ended up spending only $34 million on the national launch campaign (much less than is spent on other new-car launches) yet generated $3 billion in retail sales.

Altoids provides yet another example of creative marketing. The British breath mint has been around since the 1800s but was introduced to the United States in a small, focused campaign that started in Seattle with billboards, postcards, and creative ads in alternative newspapers. The company tested in individual markets and learned what worked before moving on. By understanding the market for its small category, Altoids has built a brand that generates $125 million in sales annually while spending less than $12 million per year on advertising.

A lean launch can work even for long-standing brands that need reinvigorating. With a controversial product to sell and severe limits on where it could advertise, Lucky Strike approached potential customers on a direct, emotional level. Understanding that most smokers feel like second-class citizens these days, the company went to several major cities and offered a hot cup of coffee and a chair to smokers forced to stand outside their office buildings in cold weather. As a result, brand sales increased for the first time in many years.

Erecting Stage Gates

To ensure a successful product launch, only products with real potential for specific markets should make it to the launch stage. And once they have reached that stage, they need marketing campaigns that are aligned with their sales potential. In fact, most companies could increase their launch success rates by 50 percent or even more by getting the right product to the right consumer at a cost that is in line with the product's sales potential and with a clear and consistent message.

We recommend that companies erect stage gates—specific points in the concept-to-launch process—where a project that isn't panning out can be stopped. Too often projects that lack real promise assume a life of their own, eating up time and resources before someone finally puts them out of their misery. There are a number of organizational reasons for this: the pressure on brand managers to score big is one. But perhaps the quickest way to avoid the problem, short of major organizational change, is to call for a "go-no-go" decision at three specific stages in the product launch process. If a new product doesn't meet the next gate's requirements, it doesn't go forward.

The first gate must appear early on, after the concept development stage. At this time, the target market for the product should be clearly identified, along with a realistic plan for reaching that market and a rough estimate of marketing costs for different targets. The brand manager should also have investigated channel requirements—for example, what supermarkets will require for placing the product—as well as estimated the initial sales volume.

The next gate would come after the commercialization model has been developed. To proceed, the brand manager must demonstrate that the product can realistically deliver on its claim and that there are plans for reaching consumers at multiple points and for creating excitement about the product before it's on the shelves.

The last gate would arise at the point of a large-scale commercial launch, when it should be clear that there is a compelling marketing plan in place to reach targeted subsegments, a plan for merchandising the product so that it stands out among others in the store, and a plan for meeting all channel requirements with risks accounted for.

*   *   *

Launching a new product is tougher today than ever. Retailers are more demanding, and large media campaigns can cost several times what they did five years ago, yet produce less. Television advertising no longer ensures success with consumers who are inundated with too many channels, too much clutter, and a confusing variety of products. Successful launches need

- a compelling reason for consumers to buy the product

- a launch budget that is aligned with the product's true market potential

- good timing and a precise marketing plan

- an internal process to kill bad ideas early—as soon as failure is obvious and before it's too late

By setting up clear stage gates, by better understanding consumers and where to reach them, and by candidly assessing a new product's category dynamics and target audience, brand managers can greatly improve their chances of profitability.

To survive, your company must demonstrate a positive net present value for investments in new-product launches. Our approach reduces shareholders' risk by eliminating unnecessary ad and trade spending and by emphasizing creative, less expensive, and more efficient strategies for marketing. Imagine: smarter, more exciting marketing plans; higher success rates with lower investment risk; and a highly profitable portfolio of innovative new products.

This article was first published in July 2002.

Breaking Out of China's Value Trap

Hubert Hsu and Jim Hemerling

China continues to represent an enormous opportunity for consumer goods companies. With an economy seven times larger than it was 20 years ago, the country is undergoing the greatest economic expansion ever witnessed—anytime, anywhere. It is already the largest market for washing machines and mobile phones, the second largest for beer, and the third largest for carbonated soft drinks.

That growth shows no sign of slowing as consumers' disposable incomes keep rising. With the full package of World Trade Organization benefits to kick in over the next few years, industries will continue to expand at rates several times those in more developed markets. And although highly regulated industries—such as telecommunications and financial services—must devote significant time and resources to cultivating and managing government relationships, consumer goods companies can spend more of their energy on business because they are among the least regulated in China.

No wonder multinational companies are encouraged by their initial forays into China. But their early success—often a result of skimming off the most affluent consumers in the biggest cities—can create a false sense of confidence in the sustainability of their business models. Because the fastest growth in China's high-income households is expected to come from outside the largest urban areas, many companies are now trying to penetrate the mass market—and they are counting on those same business models to work for them there. (See Exhibit 1.) When they expand into new locations and categories, however, they typically run into a wall of new problems. These problems include fragmented markets, consumers, and channels; low prices

Exhibit 1   **The Fastest Growth in High-Income Households Will Occur Outside Large Cities**

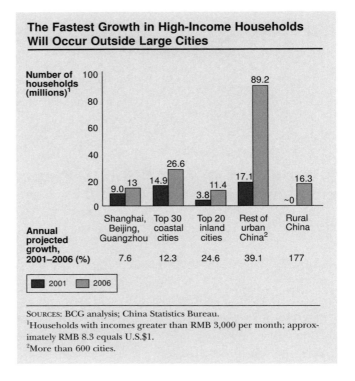

SOURCES: BCG analysis; China Statistics Bureau.
[1]Households with incomes greater than RMB 3,000 per month; approximately RMB 8.3 equals U.S.$1.
[2]More than 600 cities.

in areas beyond the large urban centers; different competitors in different regions, each employing completely different go-to-market approaches; immature distribution infrastructures and players; and extraordinary strains on organizational capabilities and infrastructure.

Most companies respond to these difficulties by allocating additional financial and human resources, only to become ensnared in the *China value trap:* the more they invest, the more they seem to lose as shareholder value drains away. Expatriate and local managers find themselves working harder and harder with no turnaround in sight.

We estimate that more than 50 percent of today's consumer-goods and retail multinationals are caught in the value trap. In the beer industry, for example, international brewers have experienced annual losses that run into tens of millions of dollars, on top of hundreds of millions in write-offs from failed investments. Moreover, the problems occur across many sectors, such as packaged food and beverages, personal care, household chemicals, consumer durables, and retail groceries.

A few leading companies, however, are emerging from this trap with remarkable alacrity, and they are developing large, profitable positions across a range of markets. (See Exhibit 2.) Conventional wisdom asserts that the key to success in China is a combination of low costs and low prices. Of course, those advantages are crucial. But a more dynamic and sophisticated model is needed in a market as complex and varied as China's. The companies that accelerate quickly out of the trap all pay close and early attention to scale, costs, and prices, but they also focus on local market insights and think creatively about resource deployment.

The Success Model Begins with a Virtuous Cycle

We've identified the collective strategies required to break out of the value trap as the *China success model.* (See Exhibit 3.) These strategies don't work independently. Rather, their power lies in their integrated nature and

Exhibit 2 **Some Companies Escape the Value Trap Quickly, Whereas Others Remain There Indefinitely**

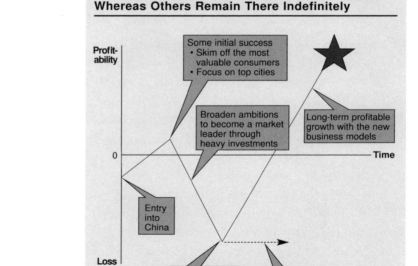

SOURCE: BCG analysis.

Exhibit 3   **The China Success Model**

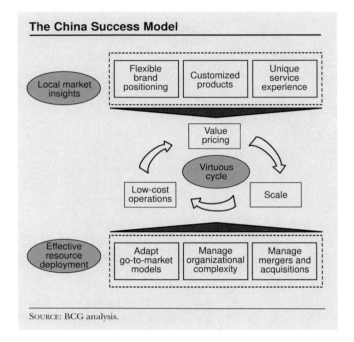

SOURCE: BCG analysis.

the ways in which they complement one another. The value trap, then, may be hard to avoid. But if a company prepares ahead of time or changes course once it is snared, it will find a way out. Indeed, the approach it employs will have a lasting impact on its business trajectory—in both the severity of the losses it experiences and the speed with which it escapes the trap. What follows is a closer look at the components of the China success model.

Value Pricing and Scale. With a national savings rate of more than 30 percent, China is famous for the frugality of its citizens. To attract value-conscious shoppers, successful local companies focus on the high-volume, lower-price-point segments. Huiyuan in juices and Sanxiao in toothbrushes, for example, price their products more than 20 percent below those of the leading multinational brands and, as a result, dominate the mass market. To compete with these successful local players, many of which have also improved their product quality and positioning, global companies must proactively cut prices. Lower prices will help deepen penetration into the mass market, which in turn will provide scale benefits to support additional pricing and value-enhancement strategies.

Tingyi, a Taiwanese company, has captured the market for packaged noodles by being the value and price leader in the premium segment. Leveraging its scale, it has built its own sales and distribution (S&D) network, which includes more than 300 sales offices across China, serving nearly 34,000 retailers directly. The remaining retail outlets are serviced through distributors, who provide logistics, and wholesalers, who sell to remote locations. That approach has allowed Tingyi to build strong relationships with its retailers and, as a result, dominate their shelves. The brand frequently commands as much as half the total space allocated to the category. Having established its S&D system, Tingyi has now embarked on an aggressive program of value improvement (larger package sizes), product extensions (an economy-priced noodle brand), and category expansions (ready-to-drink beverages and snacks).

Low-Cost Operations. When global companies focus on value pricing and scale, they frequently complain about low margins. Often, the problem is that they haven't fully explored how truly low-cost their operations could be. Most companies could significantly reduce their costs in at least three ways: by ensuring that economies of scale are fully exploited, by localizing cost structures to benefit from China's favorable factor costs, and by increasing their focus on the parts of the business that deliver real value to consumers and eliminating or reducing those that do not.

Contrary to what many multinational companies claim, our experience doesn't support the notion that local companies enjoy significant structural advantages. Some may discover small advantages by locating in lower-cost regions within China, but in relative terms, the savings are small.

Most multinationals believe they can't reduce costs by much more than 5 or 10 percent. We believe the opportunity is often more than 20 percent and possibly as high as 40 percent. When lowering costs, however, such companies need to ensure that their Chinese operations continue to leverage useful experiences and processes from the worldwide system, while they also develop local management capabilities and a business model that is relevant to serving the Chinese market. For example, when Colgate discovered Sanxiao's 30 percent cost advantage in toothbrush production and realized it would take significant time and resources to narrow the gap, it acquired the company. Now it not only owns the Chinese toothbrush market with more than 50 percent volume share, but it also uses the low-cost facility as an international sourcing center.

Local Market Insights: Understanding the Chinese Consumer

China poses an enormous challenge to multinational consumer-goods and retail companies when it comes to gaining insight into its local markets. The wide-ranging differences across the country—with its 600-plus cities, seven major dialects, and 80 or so spoken "tongues," not to mention its huge disparities in education and income—are made even more daunting by the severe inaccuracy or lack of published data. Rather than rely solely on market research, successful companies get out and talk directly with channel partners, competitors, and consumers. They also tap into the direct experience of local managers, whose insights into the subtleties of local lifestyles and preferences help the companies tailor products to meet local demand.

Flexible Brand Positioning. Multinational companies often view Chinese consumers only in the context of their global brands. Although such brands provide many advantages, they also bring with them many constraints, especially when it comes to positioning, icons, and messages. Chinese consumers still admire Western products, but they are more inclined to shop for brands they feel serve their specific needs. For example, Shiseido long ago discovered that many Chinese consumers believe that Asian skin is significantly different from the skin of non-Asians. Acting on that insight, the Japanese company established an early lead in the fast-growing cosmetics categories by noting in its advertising that its products are designed specifically for Asians.

Customized Products. The challenge of offering localized products is made harder by the fact that consumer preferences vary considerably within China. What sells in the chic environs of Shanghai might be rejected in rural communities. That's why Tingyi tailors its products to regional tastes, marketing sweeter flavors in Shanghai and saltier flavors in the northeast region. Supported by a highly sophisticated regional-production capability, the company is then able to revise its formulation continually in order to meet changing tastes, which brings it even closer to consumers.

Unique Service Experience. Chinese consumers also place a high value on superior service. That is an area in which multinationals can gain an advantage because local companies often find it difficult to deliver even the most basic service. KFC and McDonald's, for example, leveraged their global capabilities to deliver a consistently high-quality service experience that stands in stark contrast to the indifferent service typical in competing local restaurants.

Leading Chinese companies are beginning to catch up, however, and some are offering very high standards of service. Haier, for example, differentiated itself from both local and global competitors by offering a national 24-hour hotline for its appliances. Furthermore, it extended the concept to its channel partners, proactively servicing retailers to support sales, promotion, and marketing. Those actions have contributed to making Haier number one in China's appliance market.

Effective Resource Deployment

In a country as vast as China, resource deployment can be a complex issue. Like leaders in combat, business leaders must first decide which battles to fight, the optimal configuration of forces to use, and how best to deploy those forces to break through competitive positions. In short, they must adapt their go-to-market models for each regional market. Then they need to organize to ensure that those resources are not overwhelmed by the ensuing complexity of battle. Clear lines of communication and supply, as well as effective processes and policies, are vital to making certain that the troops at the front are aligned and equipped. Leaders must also decide whether to align their forces with others and how to orchestrate that deployment. Mergers, acquisitions, and alliances—together with effective integration plans—are often critical to building scale and capabilities. Although effective resource deployment can seem difficult, many companies in China are already making great progress.

Adapt go-to-market models. Large cities account for a relatively small, albeit very attractive, share of the market in most consumer categories today. What's more, future income growth will be highest outside those cities. Sooner or later, most multinational companies will decide to expand beyond their initial beachheads to tap into the vast potential of the rest of the country. (See Exhibit 4.) But once they encounter less sophisticated consumers, new competitors, immature distribution infrastructures, fragmented channels, and woefully inadequate data and information, just how many business models will they need? Clearly, one model can't work for every area. Companies will need to customize products, distribution, advertising, and promotions. But that doesn't mean that each city requires its own unique model.

We recently helped one of the largest packaged-goods companies in China reassess its business model across the more than 600 cities it served—

Exhibit 4

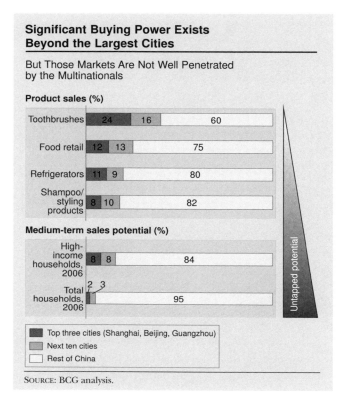

**Significant Buying Power Exists
Beyond the Largest Cities**

But Those Markets Are Not Well Penetrated
by the Multinationals

Product sales (%)

Toothbrushes	24	16	60
Food retail	12	13	75
Refrigerators	11	9	80
Shampoo/styling products	8	10	82

Medium-term sales potential (%)

High-income households, 2006	8	8	84
Total households, 2006	2	3	95

Untapped potential

■ Top three cities (Shanghai, Beijing, Guangzhou)
▨ Next ten cities
☐ Rest of China

SOURCE: BCG analysis.

nearly every urban center in the country. First, we segmented the market into city clusters with similar characteristics, winding up with a much more manageable number. Then we devised a go-to-market model for each cluster, which included channel priorities, media and promotion strategies, sales force deployment, as well as logistics models. Along the way, we identified certain regions that were simply unprofitable to serve and devised exit strategies. The exercise had a significant impact on the top and bottom lines, and it allowed the client to focus scarce resources on its most important geographic markets and channels.

Huiyuan, the leading local juice company, provides another good example. Unlike most packaged-goods companies, it eschews a diverse brand portfolio in favor of collecting most of its products under a single brand umbrella. That strategy simplifies marketing, advertising, and distribution; in addition, it enables the company to enjoy significant marketing scale advantages. What's more, the approach allows Huiyuan to enter new categories—such as packaged juice drinks—that it can introduce under the established umbrella brand and distribution network. As a result, the company has been able to achieve a profitable growth trajectory while maintaining its leadership position.

Manage organizational complexity. Expansion will inevitably increase organizational complexity because the new cities that have a growing mass market will be smaller and channels and distributors more fragmented. Expanding an initial beachhead market to 10 or 20 cities typically results in an exponential increase in the number of staff, distributors, and customers. Left unmanaged, these factors result in overwhelming organizational complexity.

When expatriate and local managers underestimate that complexity—as happens all too frequently—they find themselves spending more and more time on the road working longer and longer hours to deal with mounting operational problems in one market after another. Companies can make this process considerably easier by codifying standard processes and procedures using good management-information systems. In nascent Chinese markets, simple approaches are frequently just as effective as the sophisticated ones that multinational companies adopt in more developed markets.

For instance, a well-managed S&D network is critical, but China's market complexities cause many companies to struggle with even modest expansions. One of the few exceptions to this is PepsiCo's beverage division. The division realized that its core global processes could be just as effective in China as they are elsewhere, but success would depend on careful implementation.

Therefore, PepsiCo has piloted selected processes in a few key regional markets in order to customize them for China. These sales tools are then codified in manuals and reinforced across all of the company's teams. Global companies such as Pepsi-Co have found that a profitable pilot can be a persuasive tool for convincing Chinese managers to adopt a new system.

PepsiCo's continued success is also based on constant process renewal. To encourage innovation, it gives its supervisors significant decision-making power. Twice a year, the company organizes a national conference to bring its sales managers up to date on the latest S&D information and to share local best practices. Managerial freedom, however, is tempered by a rigorous monitoring system that entails regular evaluations by internal teams as well as third parties on key performance indicators. With these strategies, PepsiCo has rapidly and economically built a deep and expansive S&D network and gained significant share compared with Coca-Cola.

Manage mergers and acquisitions. Reluctant to relinquish any management control in this strategically important market, many companies opt for organic growth in China, despite its many—often unique—challenges. Yet the creative use of mergers and acquisitions can often be a more effective way to escape the value trap. Rather than buying a local brand simply for its products and volume, companies should consider the broader role that the acquired company could play. It could help establish a low-cost production base, for instance, or provide a mass-market S&D system for the accelerated expansion of a global product portfolio. In addition, it could offer the freedom to market a local brand—enhanced with global product technologies but free from global brand restrictions—to a huge market of price-sensitive Chinese consumers.

Nevertheless, mergers and acquisitions can involve risks that are unique to China. Due diligence for even a medium-sized acquisition could (and probably should) take months to complete. What's more, given the complex structure of government in provincial China, it is vital to use a facilitator with solid knowledge of the region. Finally, in the postmerger integration phase, it is easy to overlook the inherent differences in the operating models of acquirer and target. Companies must guard against adding layers of expenses that transform otherwise successful low-cost businesses into general-and-administrative-loaded failures.

Realizing China's Potential

As some nimble multinationals are proving, it is possible to reduce the inevitable growing pains of expansion in China and quickly return to profitability. To realize your true potential in China, start by assessing your organization's position today in relation to where you want to go and how soon you need to get there. Answering the following questions will help you guide that effort:

- Where do you stand today in relation to the value trap? Are you confident that your business in China will be in a fundamentally more advantaged position within a year?

- Have you factored in all the complexities that are inherent in your expansion plan? Have you underestimated the challenges and investments required?

- Are you developing a sufficiently deep understanding of the Chinese consumer in order to position your brands and customize your products and services?

- Do you know how to lower your operating costs by 20 to 40 percent in order to support a value-pricing strategy?

- Do you know in detail how you will adapt your go-to-market model as you start to expand beyond your initial efforts?

- Do you have the right organization, performance discipline, and processes to support your expanding business model?

- How would a merger, acquisition, or alliance help you climb out of the value trap more quickly? Has your organization explored all the creative options? Are you aware of the challenges and risks inherent in the postmerger integration?

The China value trap is real. Many companies are caught in it today and have seen significant shareholder value destroyed. If your company hasn't fallen into the trap yet, chances are it will soon. And once caught, it may seem like quicksand, because the harder you try to escape, the deeper you'll sink. It takes vision, creative strategy, courage, and precise implementation to break out of the value trap. Are you prepared for the challenge?

This article was first published in August 2002.

Dancing with the 800-Pound Gorilla

Marin Gjaja, Alexander Lintner, and Henry M. Vogel

Wal-Mart, the world's largest retailer—as well as largest company—poses an unprecedented threat to grocery channels everywhere. It has been relentlessly adding new stores, penetrating new markets, and leveraging its successful strategy for selling general merchandise to boost grocery sales, market share, and competitive advantage. As it grows and acquires its way toward stronger positions in North America and the world, its lower costs and economically advantaged formats are transforming the consumer value equation. The world has never known a company with such ambition, capability, and momentum.

Wal-Mart's U.S. grocery sales have skyrocketed from $10 billion to more than $45 billion in little over a decade—a 14.6 percent real annual growth rate. We project these sales to reach nearly $70 billion by 2005. (See Exhibit 1.) If Wal-Mart can find the right entry vehicles, it aspires to expand in Japan, Western Europe, and many developing countries. To be sure, its march across the United States—and the rest of the world—shows no signs of slowing down.

In its wake, Wal-Mart has left a trail of shuttered grocery stores. Surviving retailers in the United States face squeezed margins, diminished traffic, and a reduced share of grocery purchases. The list of retailers that have sold out or merged with others in the past ten years includes American Stores, Dominick's, Fred Meyer, Giant of Maryland, Hannaford Brothers, Randalls, Seessel's, Stop & Shop, Tom Thumb, and Vons. Retailers that have declared bankruptcy through Chapter 7 or Chapter 11 include Big V, Bruno's, Eagle Foods, Furr's, Grand Union, Homeland, Jitney-Jungle, Kmart, and Pathmark.

Wal-Mart's rapid rise to the top of the grocery industry is undoubtedly the greatest challenge that retailers and packaged goods companies have ever faced. As one retailer put it, "Wal-Mart's entry transforms grocery markets into war zones." For manufacturers, the chain is a formidable negotiating partner because it holds down prices and has gained a significant influence on consumers' perceptions of brand value. According to one senior manufacturing executive, "Wal-Mart has become the 800-pound gorilla in the grocery aisle, and you have to dance with it. The trick is to follow its lead yet think a step ahead, so it doesn't crush your toes. It's not easy."

Daunting as that challenge seems, it isn't insurmountable. Many manufacturers have thrived by serving Wal-Mart. A few competing grocery chains in the United States have also done exceptionally well. In benchmarking the U.S. grocery industry, we found that Safeway, Ahold USA, Publix Super

Exhibit 1

Wal-Mart's Grocery Sales Are Soaring

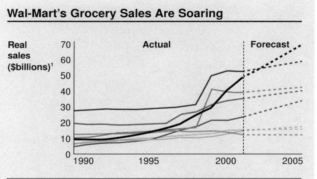

		Real CAGR (%)	
		1990–2001	2002–2005
—	Wal-Mart	14.6	9.5
—	Kroger	5.9	3.0
—	Albertson's	12.1	2.0
—	Safeway	5.2	3.5
—	Ahold USA	13.5	9.5
—	Delhaize America	6.7	3.5
—	Publix	6.7	2.0
—	Winn-Dixie	0.1	0.5

"We are bringing Wal-Mart's traditional philosophy of great quality at the lowest price to food."
        —Doug Degn, executive vice president of food merchandising

SOURCES: Compustat; company financial filings; Trade Dimensions; Value Line; U.S. Bureau of Labor Statistics; BCG estimates and analysis. [1]Estimated total U.S. grocery sales (supermarkets, groceries at supercenters, clubs, and convenience stores) for indicated retailers. Real sales numbers are stated in 2001 dollars.

Markets, and Kroger actually achieved higher cash-flow margins than Wal-Mart. But on other key dimensions, such as asset turns, supermarket sales per store, sales per employee, and total EBITDA per store and per square foot, Wal-Mart leads most traditional grocery chains. (See Exhibits 2 and 3.)

To live with—even *succeed* with—Wal-Mart as your customer or competitor, it helps to understand how the chain achieved its hegemony and how it uses it to trounce the competition. If Wal-Mart is in your market now, you'll need to know how it competes; if it's not there yet, it probably will be soon, and you'll need to assess when and in what form it will arrive. The goal is to craft a strategy that allows you to coexist with Wal-Mart while leveraging your advantages. Successful retailers will anticipate Wal-Mart's entrance, slow

Exhibit 2

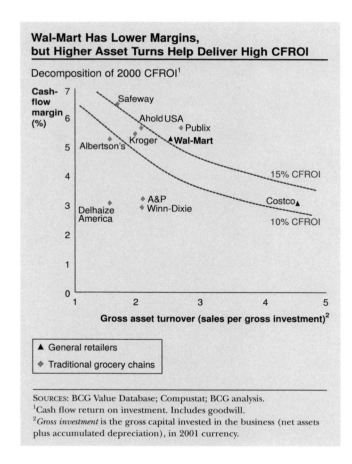

Wal-Mart Has Lower Margins, but Higher Asset Turns Help Deliver High CFROI

Decomposition of 2000 CFROI[1]

SOURCES: BCG Value Database; Compustat; BCG analysis.
[1]Cash flow return on investment. Includes goodwill.
[2]*Gross investment* is the gross capital invested in the business (net assets plus accumulated depreciation), in 2001 currency.

Exhibit 3   **Wal-Mart Has More Profitable Stores and More Productive Employees Than Traditional Groceries**

	Average employees per store (FTE)	Estimated supermarket sales[1]		Estimated total EBITDA[2]		Average sales per employee ($thousands)[3]
		Per store ($millions)	Per square foot ($)	Per store ($millions)	Per square foot ($)	
Kroger	95	19.2	529	1.4	31	216
Safeway	75	20.1	556	2.2	58	290
Albertson's	88	17.6	505	1.4	40	251
Ahold USA	83	19.4	488	1.8	45	225
Delhaize America	45	10.4	359	0.8	28	228
Publix	106	21.3	535	1.5	37	209
Winn-Dixie	76	11.4	293	0.3	7	149
A&P	76	16.5	521	0.9	28	280
Costco club stores	150	62.5	1,141	4.9	42	623
Wal-Mart Super-centers	**182**	**29.6**	**484**	**8.5**	**54**	**434**

SOURCES: *Progressive Grocer;* Trade Dimensions; company filings; analyst reports; literature search; BCG estimates and analysis.

NOTE: Data are from 2001.

[1]Estimates include only supermarket-equivalent sales (those items sold in a traditional supermarket format) and selling space.

[2]Estimates include total company EBITDA and selling space (supermarket and nonsupermarket items).

[3]Estimates are for total sales and employees, including those in non-supermarket formats, such as standalone drugstores and fuel centers.

its expansion, and exploit its weaknesses. Winning manufacturers will discover ways to grow their Wal-Mart business more profitably as they extend and reinvest in their brands to reinforce their position.

Why Wal-Mart Leads the U.S. Industry

When Wal-Mart entered the grocery business, the U.S. food industry was a highly fragmented yet stable market. In most cities, two chains faced off, surrounded by many local independents. Competition tolerated weak performance. But in short order, Wal-Mart turned the industry upside down. Sam Walton, founder of Wal-Mart, once said that his goal was to lower the cost of living. To fulfill this mission, he built a business that achieved unmatched performance in five areas: scale economies, advantaged formats, Every Day Low Prices (EDLP), category focus, and continuous improvement.

Scale Economies. Even before Wal-Mart entered the grocery business, it had many scale advantages over its competitors, particularly in the following areas:

Procurement. Wal-Mart clearly achieves the best terms and conditions with its suppliers in most categories, especially in the United States. And if it successfully moves to global procurement as it expands internationally, it will be able to extend this advantage to other markets as well.

Distribution and Logistics. Unlike most other retailers in the United States, Wal-Mart invests in and controls its own vertically integrated supply chain. It is also working to build similar networks in the new markets it has recently entered. Wal-Mart leverages this scale to maximize drop sizes and route densities (a large part of distribution costs). It also invests in integrated IT systems and works with suppliers to eliminate inefficiencies, improve order accuracy, shrink order-to-delivery cycles, and reduce inventories.

Marketing and General Administration. With more than $200 billion in total sales, Wal-Mart is five times the size of its nearest grocery competitor, which allows it to achieve significant scale in overhead expenses. As a global brand, it is also able to reap scale advantages in advertising and marketing.

Wal-Mart's expansion into food has extended those economies of scale even further.

Advantaged Formats. The supercenter format—which borrows from the European hypermarket concept of selling both groceries and general merchandise—has been critical to Wal-Mart's success in food retailing. The economics of supercenters are far superior to those of traditional stores because supercenters are bigger and can spread fixed costs over more sales. Although the grocery portion of a Wal-Mart supercenter is only about 61,000 square feet (bigger than most traditional grocery stores, but not that much bigger), the entire store averages about 185,000 square feet. An even more important factor is traffic. Consumers visit grocery stores more often than they do general discount stores. Wal-Mart's low food prices entice customers to visit its supercenters even more frequently; and when they do, they're likely to buy high-margin general merchandise. In essence, Wal-Mart uses food as a "low-margin leader" to drive traffic, which results in faster inventory turns and greater profits overall per square foot.

Wal-Mart is also expanding its successful Sam's Club format and experimenting with new concepts, most notably the Neighborhood Market. Neighborhood Markets look like smaller, traditional supermarkets and are designed to "fill in" areas between supercenters or to compete in dense urban locations, where space constraints make supercenters impractical. Because these stores are less crowded and closer to customers' homes, they eliminate some of the disadvantages of supercenters that consumers complain about. But although the stores are smaller, they still benefit from Wal-Mart's advantaged procurement, distribution, and logistics infrastructure. We estimate that Neighborhood Markets have a six-point margin advantage over traditional grocery stores.

EDLP Pricing. Wal-Mart uses the savings from its lower-cost business model to support consistently lower prices on a wide range of products. Its message, displayed prominently in bold letters on the outside of almost every store, is clear: "Always low prices!" When Wal-Mart enters a new market—anywhere in the world—the average price of key grocery items drops considerably. In fact, slashing prices is one of the first actions the company takes after acquiring other retailers. For example, in Germany it rolled back prices in several chains it purchased 10 to 30 percent below what its competitors charged on approximately 1,700 SKUs—about 15 percent of the total product assortment.

Category Focus. Wal-Mart focuses on categories that attract high-value consumers, such as large families. It features products with long shelf lives—paper goods and cleaning products, for example—because families purchase them in bulk. Wal-Mart also employs a strategy introduced by Carrefour and other hypermarkets in Europe: it focuses on food staples and high-premium categories (such as dairy products, confectionery goods, and health and beauty aids) so that its low prices will demonstrate real consumer value. And it has been increasing its investment in its own brands—Great Value and Sam's Choice—as well as in newly acquired "premium" private-label brands, such as White Cloud. The power of Wal-Mart's private-label brands has yet to reach its full potential.

Continuous Improvement. Many companies pay lip service to continuous improvement, but Wal-Mart has a passion for it. The chain weaves the concept into the very fabric of its business system by using its vast network of stores to run frequent experiments. As a result, it moves up the experience curve much faster and more consistently than its competitors.

Perhaps the most notable example is Wal-Mart's dramatic improvement in its perishables offering. The quality of fresh produce and meat is a critical factor for most grocery shoppers, and Wal-Mart's customers had perceived the retailer to be inferior in this area for years. After much experimentation and investment, however, Wal-Mart has improved its delivery of perishables to such an extent that its customers no longer feel they are compromising when they shop there.

Competing to Win

Without doubt, Wal-Mart's meteoric growth has been hard on the competition. The first victims are usually small, independent grocers, whose customers succumb to the siren song of Wal-Mart's low prices. Given the razor-thin margins in food retailing, even slight shifts in traffic or small declines in margins can be a fatal blow. Although larger players may sometimes experience an increase in sales and share when the independents close their doors, the uptick for them doesn't last long. As Wal-Mart continues to lower costs, slash prices, and add stores, they begin to feel the pain, too. (See Exhibit 4.)

But Wal-Mart isn't invincible. The first step in competing effectively with the gorilla is to improve efficiency and reduce costs. To cut costs, retailers must build and reinforce local scale and reduce supply chain expenses, inventories, and operating overhead. Once Wal-Mart enters the trade area of a given store, sales will likely suffer for at least three months while customers try the new retailer. That's the time to lower prices on basic items to win those customers back from Wal-Mart and away from the weaker competitors that will go out of business.

But these efforts are just a ticket to stay at the dance. In order to win, retailers will need to leverage their advantages.

Location and Local Market Knowledge. All retailing is local. Competitors that succeed against Wal-Mart capitalize on local share positions, brand recognition, and convenient sites in attractive areas. They exit unprofitable stores or subscale markets. When they enter new areas, they expand in concentric circles around their core markets, where they understand the local consumers and can extend their brands. Such expansion also allows them to leverage their supply chain infrastructure. H.E. Butt (H-E-B), for example, has defended its position by reinvesting in markets where it is dominant and by selectively expanding out from its core.

In Europe, some grocery players—notably Tesco in the United Kingdom and Lidl's Kaufland in Germany—have been able to beat back competition

Exhibit 4

Wal-Mart's Entry Eliminates Independents and Squeezes Major Players

It accelerates the demise of independents . . .

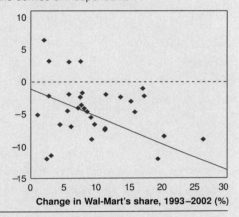

. . . and puts pressure on many top players

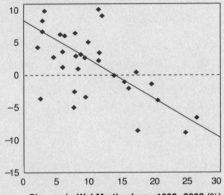

SOURCES: ACNielsen; Scantrack; Trade Dimensions; Market Scope; BCG analysis.
NOTE: Each symbol represents the average change in market share for independents (top box) and for the top three players excluding Wal-Mart (bottom box) in a local market area. Wal-Mart's share gain in those same markets is represented on the horizontal axis. The regression lines show the correlation between Wal-Mart's share gain and the change in share of the other players in a given market.

from hypermarkets and defend against Wal-Mart's recent acquisition of local players. They did it by leveraging such local strengths as savvy product assortments in individual stores and superior product availability. They also exploited Wal-Mart's relatively weak economies of scale and lack of infrastructure in Europe—especially in Germany. In Spain, hypermarket growth has begun to plateau because consumers find these stores too crowded and too distant from home.

Differentiated Formats. Some innovative retailers are competing successfully against Wal-Mart with even lower prices or better service by doing the following:

- Establishing "price impact," or "dollar," stores, which provide narrower product assortments, fewer national brands, and lower-cost service, enabling the retailers to charge less than Wal-Mart

- Achieving "destination status" in important categories, such as fresh meat; produce; gourmet, organic, or ethnic products; and home-meal replacement

- Building traffic with brands that Wal-Mart doesn't carry and stretching the price pyramid within categories to enable better positioning

- Investing in new service concepts, such as convenience stores or pantry sections, online shopping and home delivery, ethnic formats, or "retail-tainment" services

Other U.S. players—Meijer, for example, and more recently Target—are actually matching Wal-Mart's successful supercenter format.

Tailored Assortment. Offering the right product assortment remains one of the critical success factors in the grocery business. Although Wal-Mart's range of products is very broad, it isn't always perfect, and "back to basics" can be a viable strategy to exploit this weakness. But figuring out what the basics are is no small challenge given the increasing variety of products and the heterogeneity of today's consumers. Nonetheless, new systems and business processes can help micromanage individual store plan-o-grams—the "maps" that determine which products are on which shelves—and align the product assortment and price points with local demographics and shopping preferences. Becoming a true neighborhood market may help preempt Wal-Mart.

Precision Pricing and Promotions. In some ways, Wal-Mart has become predictable in its pricing and promotions. Its EDLP model stands out from the "high-low promotions" that many retailers use, but it's not best for all products. Categories in which consumers expect to find sales, for example, or categories that are highly impulsive or seasonal don't lend themselves to a strict across-the-board application of EDLP. What's more, our research indicates that consumers don't actually remember the prices of many grocery products. That means retailers don't necessarily have to match Wal-Mart's pricing or be the lowest on *all* products. Better to discover which products determine *your* customers' price impressions in *your* stores and manage those specific prices.

Frequent-shopper programs (FSPs) can help in this effort. By now, most U.S. grocers have invested in them and, as a result, are sitting on a gold mine of information about their customers' actual behavior and preferences. However, few retailers have leveraged those data effectively. But when they do, they will discover a powerful weapon against Wal-Mart. New data-mining techniques and technologies for communicating with individual customers allow retailers to execute true segment-of-one promotions and pricing. Instead of offering moderately low prices on everything to everyone all the time, retailers could provide deep discounts on specific products tailored to individual preferences when the customers want those products. Or they could offer other loyalty-building incentives that go beyond one-time product discounts—cumulative loyalty rebates based on total purchases, for instance—or nonprice incentives such as special services or perks. And since Wal-Mart has disavowed FSPs, retailers that successfully employ these programs stand to gain a point of differentiation and advantage.

Sales Associates Committed to the Local Market. Although Wal-Mart focuses on the most value-conscious consumers, that's not everyone, on every shopping trip. Some consumers are willing to pay for better service. Traditional players such as Publix and H-E-B, for example, and higher-end retailers such as EatZi's and Whole Foods Market have differentiated themselves by the superior service their employees provide.

Perhaps the best example of a retailer that is competing successfully against Wal-Mart by pulling all of these levers is Tesco. Since Wal-Mart's entry in the United Kingdom, Tesco has redoubled its efforts and actually raised its market share. It did this by installing a "Step Change" team to lower costs and increase responsiveness to customers. It invested the savings in lower prices and reinforced a good-better-best pricing architecture with a range of products under its own label. Finally, it developed and expanded new formats, such as its Metro stores in urban locations, which customers use for "top-off" shopping. It has even introduced its own supercenters.

Tesco has also sharpened its customer-specific pricing, and its price-communication and promotional tactics. For example, by mining its Clubcard FSP data, it can segment its customers into a multitude of discrete groups on the basis of sociodemographic factors, shopping behavior (such as types of products purchased, frequency of trips, average purchase amount, and total amount spent), and response rates to previous offers. As a result, in its quarterly mailings to more than 10 million households, Tesco can have as many as half a million customized variations of the information, coupons, and special promotions it offers.

Dancing the Wal-Mart Tango

Being a supplier to Wal-Mart can be as challenging as competing against it. But it can also produce spectacular results. Here's how most successful manufacturers do it:

Partner to reduce supply chain costs. Wal-Mart is famous for "partnering" with individual suppliers when it wants to improve its margins or drive growth in a given category. It's better to seize the initiative and proactively reduce costs than to have a gorilla breathing down your neck. Suppliers should take the following steps:

- Work with Wal-Mart's operations group to identify ways to reduce inventories and costs. The largest opportunities are typically to be found in shrinking order-to-delivery cycles, streamlining ordering, and reducing inaccuracies.

- Provide more efficient case and packaging configurations that are easier to merchandise—such as Pretty Darn Quicks. (But suppliers should also be aware that Wal-Mart may try to shift costs to them.)

- Leverage Wal-Mart's point-of-sale data to improve product assortment, demand forecasting, and replenishment.

- Build monitoring tools to detect stockouts, and develop rapid replenishment systems to reduce their frequency.

Optimize EDLP. Although it's true that Wal-Mart's customers are more price conscious—and therefore its products have higher demand elasticity—not all Wal-Mart products and not all of Wal-Mart's formats and stores are the same. Suppliers need to understand the cost structure and true demand elasticity of every key product in every Wal-Mart store. The trick is to find the optimal price that will drive the maximum amount of sales and profit for both parties. We call it *precision pricing*, and it is a tremendous opportunity to benefit from EDLP. But it requires close collaboration if both parties are to realize the greatest profits. (See "Recovering the Pricing Opportunity," Opportunities for Action, June 2002.)

Know when to push for promotions. Wal-Mart will occasionally relax its EDLP orthodoxy. It will run temporary price rollbacks in selected categories and give in-store support to suppliers that convince the company that value will accrue from incremental volume lifts. Indeed, Wal-Mart has found that judicious use of promotions can augment its business without diminishing its EDLP positioning. To succeed with this strategy, suppliers must understand the consumer value equation—including the non-price-related elements, such as in-store conditions—and look for cross-selling approaches that can drive sales in individual stores.

Become a category master. Wal-Mart will offer "category captain" status to a select number of suppliers with which it will share additional data and from which it will accept input on assortment, merchandising, and space allocation. But Wal-Mart category captains must earn their stripes by demonstrating insight about Wal-Mart's customers, an understanding of the store's categories, and a near perfect knowledge of its business. Suppliers also need to appreciate the role that their categories, brands, and SKUs play in Wal-Mart's strategy. Success often requires original research among Wal-Mart's customers and creative analysis using data from Wal-Mart's store-level information system or in-store observations.

Innovate your customer marketing. Manufacturers that combine deep category insight with their understanding of Wal-Mart's customers and business systems can develop powerful products and marketing campaigns tailored for Wal-Mart. What's more, there are many ways to do this cost-effectively. One approach is to use Wal-Mart as a launching pad for new products. Given the rising cost of national media campaigns and the fact that more than 72 million people visit a Wal-Mart store every week, the company can be an effective vehicle for encouraging consumer awareness and spurring product trial. Another way to market products with Wal-Mart is to develop seasonal offerings. Yet another is to tailor national promotional campaigns by adding programming specific to Wal-Mart—such as sweepstakes for Wal-Mart customers or special in-store events.

*   *   *

You *can* dance successfully with Wal-Mart—whether you do business with it or compete against it. But it will take careful preparation, sound analysis, strategic consumer insight, a committed organization, and outstanding execution—all of which require imagination and perseverance. Companies that offer differentiated products, deliver better service, and meet their customers' needs through a more precise segmentation will curb Wal-Mart's power.

Here are some questions that retailers should ask to prepare for Wal-Mart's challenge:

- *Cost parity:* Do you know how your current, fully loaded cost position compares with Wal-Mart's? What do you need to do to achieve parity? When will you do it?

- *Local advantage:* Are you building local advantage into everything you do—marketing, product assortment, real estate, recruiting, sponsorships, and store design?

- *Customer segmentation:* Are you focusing your efforts on the 20 percent of your customers who deliver 80 percent of your profits? Do you know which households are most vulnerable to Wal-Mart and why, which are most valuable to you, how many you have lost, and what you are doing to regain their loyalty?

- *Precision pricing:* Have you prepared a pricing response to Wal-Mart—one that communicates value and leaves you with sufficient margins to survive?

Consumer products companies that supply Wal-Mart can thrive as well. The following questions will help them assess their opportunities to increase their profitability with Wal-Mart:

- *Supply chain management:* Do you drive the Wal-Mart supply-chain agenda to reduce your own costs, as well as Wal-Mart's?

- *Perfect execution:* Have you leveraged Wal-Mart's Retail Link/DSS data to optimize your store-level execution and achieve zero stock-outs, perfect orders, and optimal store-level plan-o-grams and product assortments?

- *Pricing on the profit parabola:* Have you optimized your pricing and promotion strategy (by format, store, product, and SKU) to attract the most sales, share, and profit for your business and Wal-Mart's?

- *Consumer insight:* Do you know how consumers shop for your categories and products at Wal-Mart and do you understand their unmet needs? Have you established an active testing program and used your insights to develop products and programs just for Wal-Mart?

Answering these questions will reveal opportunities to make the most of your advantages and stay half a step ahead of Wal-Mart. When you find the right answers, you will be ready to take on the gorilla.

This article was first published in September 2002.

Choice, Proliferation, and Changing Economics: Advertising at an Inflection Point

Dan Jansen and Orin Herskowitz

Digital technology is dramatically transforming the way media content is delivered. In giving consumers greater control over the content they want, as well as when and how they receive it, the technology has set off a series of complicated first- and second-order effects that go far beyond the media industry itself. Indeed, the shift has profound implications for all advertisers, but particularly for those that rely on television.

As viewing habits change, advertisers will find it harder to reach a mass audience and to measure the cost-effectiveness of their effort. That could well affect the ability of consumer products manufacturers to promote new products, potentially slowing the pace of new-product development and brand adoption. This slow-boiling revolution will eventually have an impact on most marketers.

It's not just that some consumers are already able to avoid television commercials; the growing number of ways consumers can retrieve content, store it, interact with it, and even shape it is making communication with target audiences much more complex and difficult. But one thing is certain: a period of significant change has begun.

Equally certain, greater consumer control over television is also giving birth to new opportunities. Innovative companies are using emerging technologies to reach out to consumers in ways that more directly affect their lives—making for richer and longer-lasting relationships. This is the advertising industry's inflection point. To benefit from the upside and avoid the downside, consumer companies must prepare to act quickly. The first step is to understand the evolving trends in digital technology that affect how advertisers communicate with consumers.

Coming Attractions: Greater Consumer Control

Over the past 15 years, we have seen enormous changes in the way media content is captured and stored. With set-top boxes, home media servers, MP3 jukeboxes, video-game consoles, and cell phones, consumers are adding, in effect, an array of high-capability hard drives to their homes, cars, briefcases, and even refrigerator doors and elevator walls. These devices have all become potential platforms for the media. The result has been fierce competition, much duplication, and considerable consumer choice—as well as confusion. This confusion affects any company that uses the media to advertise, since no one knows yet which platforms will prove most valuable in attracting consumers. Some people are early adopters of new platforms, but most consumers—and many businesses—are sitting tight and waiting for things to settle down. As the digital revolution intensifies, so, too, will the battle for consumers' attention.

Not only will consumers have more choice in how they receive their content, they'll also have more power to select it. In addition to the plethora of television channels already available, consumers are rapidly gaining access to regular and subscription video on demand (VOD and SVOD), digital cable, interactive TV (iTV), satellite radio and TV, and broadband Internet. Wireless may add even more channels, with next-generation cellular platforms transmitting video directly to PDAs and cell phones. The increasing degree of interactivity on these channels will allow consumers to "pull" the content they want rather than have it "pushed" on them. For all consumer companies that advertise, these forces will make the task of finding an audience and having an impact on it much more challenging.

Even more daunting for advertisers is the prospect of losing control over their messages. Digital video recorders (DVRs), such as TiVo and Sonicblue's ReplayTV, allow television viewers to store their own programs, share them with friends, and—most significantly for advertisers—skip the commercials. And ad skipping is only the beginning: wide-scale time shifting and self-programming will further derail advertisers' strategies to reach audiences. Although relatively few consumers have purchased DVRs so far, the machines' functionality will soon be widely available as consumer electronics manufacturers and satellite-cable players embed the technology in new generations of offerings. Some industry watchers predict that at least half of U.S. households will have the technology within five years.

Approximately 70 percent of existing DVR owners say they always or often fast-forward through commercials, according to NextResearch, a U.S. marketing firm. Put that statistic beside the increasing number of households with DVR capability, and suddenly the ability of a television commercial to have a cost-effective impact on a mass audience seems highly questionable. VOD, SVOD, and iTV will accelerate the trend of consumer control over media content, to the further detriment of advertisers. Satellite radio, which uses few commercials, is likely to reduce the effectiveness of yet another traditional stronghold for consumer companies.

The Implications of Consumer Control: Unbundling

Sonicblue's ReplayTV has become something of a symbol of all that is threatening the existing order. A number of broadcasters have joined the movie studios in a legal battle to pull the plug on ReplayTV because of its ability to distribute copies of cable and television programs over the Internet.

Whether this kind of distribution constitutes piracy or not, it represents a fundamental change in consumer behavior. Thanks to ReplayTV and other new devices, consumers are being retrained to think of music, TV programming, and newspaper content in a radically different way: as individual components, rather than the bundled packages the media industries put forth.

To the extent that the TV networks are major carriers of advertising, consumer companies will be especially challenged by this form of unbundling. Although audience fragmentation has rendered TV advertising increasingly costly and inefficient over the past 15 years, TV commercials remain the primary driver of demand for most consumer goods. TV ads help to build awareness and brand image, thereby supporting price premiums. But the ad skipping, time shifting, and self-programming that unbundling permits aren't the only threats to this market.

Because of unbundling, the television networks also risk being further marginalized as navigators. Since most TV shows are produced by outside companies, the networks currently provide value to consumers—and advertisers—by packaging "quality" shows into whole evenings of "free" entertainment. As DVRs disassemble these bundles and interactive electronic-programming guides (EPGs) fight to become the new navigators, the very role of a network as an advertising platform may be significantly eroded. The bottom line: the ability of networks to deliver value to advertisers is changing as you read this.

The New Promise of Next-Generation TV

Those are the threats. But what about the opportunities? Next-generation TV offerings (DVRs, VOD, SVOD, and iTV) have made television "interactive": it watches you while you watch it. In the process of interacting with the growing number of hard drives in their homes, consumers will supply vast amounts of information about themselves. Advertisers will be able to learn which programs and commercials individuals watch, which ones they skip, when they prefer to watch certain programs, and even where—upstairs or in the kitchen. Although privacy issues will still need to be addressed, the potential marketing scenarios are enticing.

As the technology spreads through middle-class households, advertisers will be able to send commercials to specific individuals—a technique known as addressable advertising. A commercial for minivans, for example, might be directed to the TV in a family's living room, while a promo for Nickelodeon is sent to the kids' bedrooms. The same technology that can send a message to a specific audience will also allow for greater ad customization. Companies have long used audience demographics to tweak the messages they deliver in advertisements, especially in the print media. With addressable advertising, it now becomes possible to adjust for age, locality, purchasing history, time of delivery, and programming tastes. Even the digital signage at live sporting events can be targeted for that night's audience. And it's not just advertisers that benefit. Commercials that are timely, relevant, and informative can be useful to consumers, especially if they also help pay for the TV programming.

In fact, addressable advertising is being tested by a number of companies today, and the prognosis looks promising. One food manufacturer, in a recent pilot, targeted its commercials to four simple demographic segments in a region: households with kids and without kids, and households with incomes below $75,000 and with incomes above $75,000. The company claims the targeting experiment proved so effective that it was willing to pay twice the usual cost per thousand impressions (CPM) to get its messages to the target segments.

Another advantage of digital technology is its ability to close the deal on the spot. With interactive TV, which is already well under way in some European countries, consumers can obtain more information or make purchases simply by hitting a button on their remote controls. The QVC home-shopping network in the United Kingdom generates about 10 percent of its sales this way.

Of course, not all products are suitable for customized messages or real-time interactivity. But they could still reach a wide audience by being placed in the content of TV programs. It's a practice that goes all the way back to the days when the characters on the *I Love Lucy* show smoked the cigarette brand of the sponsor, Philip Morris. Fast-forward to a recent episode of *Will & Grace*. One of the lead characters had become obsessed with Cher, and Mattel's new Cher doll was featured prominently in the plot. Twenty-two million people saw the show, and sales of the product benefited greatly. Other examples include Fox's *American Idol*, in which several segments of the show took place in a Ford automobile. With the abundance of channels that digital technology provides, there will be more opportunities for program producers and advertisers to create and distribute shows jointly, thereby blurring the line between advertising and entertainment. "Advertainment" will grow and become more important to advertisers.

Getting into the Game

Major changes in technology are always unsettling, especially when they have such broad implications. It is tempting to conclude that if you aren't sure of the outcome, it's better to do nothing at all. But that approach can leave money on the table or, worse, give the competition a head start. Instead, why not invest time in understanding the threats and opportunities ahead? Here are some questions and ideas to help you get started.

Do you know the cost of diminishing reach? Do you know how a decline in consumer awareness will change your launch economics? Are you vulnerable to the digital revolution? You are if your product is a mass offering with low entertainment value. Audiences will be increasingly likely to skip over your messages. Placing your product in the content of a program is one answer. The first step is to estimate the impact of consumers' greater control over TV on your specific product offerings.

Could you improve your targeting? Would you be able to pinpoint the right audience at the right price? If you sell to a differentiated audience, consider sacrificing audience size for a larger impact on particular segments. You will need to assess the greater cost of addressable advertising to determine if it is worth it.

Where should you advertise? Do you have a complete list of options? The relatively simple choices of cable versus network and local versus national will be complicated by the increasing power of EPGs and DVRs. You will want to determine the merits of broader placement through EPGs and DVRs if your commercials are likely to be skipped. It may be time to reinvent exactly what an ad is.

Is it time to change your marketing mix? If your ads are going to be skipped, and placing your product in program content or ancillary offerings (such as EPGs or DVRs) isn't possible, perhaps you should rethink the effectiveness of television. Other media and promotional strategies may work better and should play a larger role.

Are you using the right metrics? In a TV world controlled by consumers, where you can't be sure your ads are being viewed, CPMs may no longer be a good measure of reach and impact. Traditional metrics will need to be revamped and new metrics developed to connect the cost of advertising with the actual outcomes.

As consumer companies come to terms with this inflection point, they will need to look closely at the unique features of their products and customers to find creative ways to get their messages out. The market leaders are already in their second generation of experiments. It's not too early to rethink the role of TV.

This article was first published in October 2002.

Assuming Leadership: The First 100 Days

Patrick Ducasse and Tom Lutz

During his first 100 days in office, President Franklin D. Roosevelt "sent 15 messages to Congress, guided 15 major laws to enactment, delivered 10 speeches, held press conferences and cabinet meetings twice a week, conducted talks with foreign heads of state, sponsored an international conference, made all the major decisions in domestic and foreign policy, and never displayed fright or panic and rarely even bad temper."

—Arthur M. Schlesinger Jr.,
The Age of Roosevelt: The Coming of the New Deal

Most of our readers will step into a new job at some point in the next five years. Many will be recruited or promoted to the top post in their companies. Their performance during their first 100 days in office will be crucial: friends and foes alike will be watching for signs of long-term success or failure.

In 2001, just 28 percent of the CEOs at large global companies had been in office for more than five years, down sharply from 37 percent in 1999.[1] And by the end of 2001, more than half of the CEOs had been in office for less than three years. Although nearly 90 percent of CEO appointments go to internal candidates who have had long tenures with their companies, that

---

1. The statistics in this paragraph are from a survey of more than 450 large global corporations conducted in early 2002 and sponsored by Drake Beam Morin, an executive search and outplacement firm.

doesn't make the imperative to deliver a strong takeoff any less daunting. To come even close to filling FDR's shoes today, leaders will need to be highly visible, pragmatically optimistic, action oriented, and willing to listen to others' views.

We asked 20 CEOs to tell us about their first months in office: what they intended to do, what they did, what they regretted doing, and what they regretted not doing. We heard some good stories and received a lot of practical advice, such as

- "Diagnose first, decide second."

- "Follow your instincts."

- "Take notes, then prioritize and act."

- "Understand that as the head person, you have only three topics: people, strategy, and values. Everything else is secondary."

- "Pick a kitchen cabinet of people you trust and use them for problem solving."

Then we asked the CEOs to consider their own advice and come up with the agenda they would follow if they could start over in their jobs today. Ten actions were consistently mentioned.

1. Assess the company's leadership team and complete your initial round of changes within the first 30 days. No group is likely to have a greater impact on the business than the team of direct reports that you put together. When forming that team, it makes sense to add a few trustworthy outsiders who will be able to help change the culture and create a sense of urgency. But don't discount old-timers. They carry the memory of the company, have years of experience, and are usually more interested in the business than in their own careers.

To choose the right people, you need to do some research and then be willing to act on your intuition. Review each candidate's record with the head of human resources, look at the data on his or her performance, and hold personal interviews with the most promising players in order to develop a sense of whom you can rely on. Your assessment should include the basics of strategy: Do they understand market turns, competitive vulnerability, and cost opportunities? What additional skills will they need and how quickly can they acquire them? The countdown to the end of the honeymoon period begins with the announcement of your appointment in the *Wall Street Journal.*

2. Communicate your vision of a better company and make sure employees understand how you will get there. It may be too early for specific details about your plans, but you should convey the basic values that will serve as your framework for making future decisions. Employees need to understand that you are sincere and competent. Answer questions honestly and don't promise miracles. This is also the time to be clear about your management style—how you will treat others and how they should treat you. Doing so will save everyone from wasting valuable energy trying to figure out how to please you.

3. Meet ten salespeople on the frontline and ask them what the company should be doing. Opening up the chain of command will introduce new sources of intelligence. Frontline people know the business inside and out. They hear all of the customers' complaints, know where all of the quality problems are, and are often able to predict a downward trend before the financial people can. Ask the salespeople what you can do to make their working lives better and what parts of their work give them satisfaction and need to be preserved. Honest engagement now can set the stage for receiving valuable information for years to come.

4. Meet with ten major customers for an outside-in view of the business. Customer meetings are an invaluable means of gathering anecdotal information about current performance, business trajectories, and any indirect competition that may be out there. Furthermore, bringing your senior people together with the senior people in your customers' companies can help forge strong bonds. Listen carefully, receive the feedback graciously, and be sure to act on valuable ideas.

5. Pay attention to personal habits. Imagine yourself projected on a 50-foot screen by a video camera. Every move you make as a leader will be subject to discussion and interpretation. That includes how early you arrive for work, how you relate to people in the hallway, how you allocate your time, and how thoroughly you prepare for meetings. This is a good time to signal the strength of your commitment by identifying one or two aspects of the company culture that you want to change and then changing them quickly. But beware of setting precedents in solving problems today that limit your range of options for finding solutions tomorrow.

6. In a turnaround situation, stop all discretionary spending until you have determined your business priorities. Cash is still king. It is critical to husband resources for major initiatives. If a business isn't performing well, you should rethink all of it—including advertising, new-product development, and the need for major operational changes. Every organization's budget supports a number of items that can be reduced or eliminated at no risk. Too often, the most important projects lack sufficient resources because money is being spent on less worthy causes. Create a short list of priorities and make sure they are well funded and carefully tracked.

7. Learn how the business creates profitability: understand leverage points and develop simple reporting metrics. Figuring out where the money comes from and where it goes can be quite difficult. And given the close scrutiny executives are subjected to today, it will be necessary to know *all* of the company's revenue-recognition policies. CEOs often delegate this task to the CFO. That can be a big mistake. A firsthand understanding of how the revenue side of the business works will help uncover hidden short-term upsides or squirreled-away reserves. It will also help identify the key indicators that employees and management look for in assessing the business. There are profit engines inside every organization—find yours and accelerate their growth.

8. Understand the problems that reside on the balance sheet and communicate them early. You get one chance to erase the mistakes of your predecessors. Identify and deal with these legacy issues immediately. Unpleasant surprises—obsolete inventory, insufficient warranty reserves, excessive goodwill, unresolved customer disputes, and festering litigation—have a way of hiding behind the numbers. Critical off-balance-sheet commitments also need to be understood, including promises made by the previous management team. A good rule of thumb is to expose everything and devise conservative principles for the future.

9. Develop the ability to detect hidden threats and opportunities. Apply Band-Aids where necessary. Keep a running list of quick hits. Quick hits might include running more profitable product promotions, negotiating an expanded agreement with a key customer, curtailing new-product development in weak categories, and launching a comprehensive productivity initiative to match a competitor's lower costs. But don't fall into the trap of trying to fix every problem in an attempt to show you are in charge. You will become so bogged down in operational details that you will lose sight of the big picture.

10. Manage the expectations of your board of directors by crafting a master plan for all of your communications and making sure the leadership team follows it consistently. "Managing upward" can be the most important part of the job. Learn to set expectations that you can exceed when the time comes. Keep everyone informed about risks and what is being done to avoid them. And make sure the management team speaks with one set of facts and conclusions.

*   *   *

Fair or not, leaders of companies (as well as countries) are closely scrutinized during their first 100 days in office. A successful first quarter not only promises more to come, it can also help further your goals, because everyone wants to back a winner. A strong report card during the first 100 days can set the tone for the next 1,000. Reread our recommendations for new CEOs. You may need them sooner than you think.

This article was first published in November 2002.

The New Luxury: Trading Up and Trading Down

Michael Silverstein and Neil Fiske

As we close this year, the prospect of a double-dip recession has brought storm clouds over consumer businesses. Retailers and manufacturers have been caught by an increase in consumer fears and a slowdown in spending. The "wealth health" that a burgeoning stock market and pulsing real estate market provided seems a distant memory for many consumers. Consequently, they are looking at discretionary purchases with a sharper eye.

But such wariness doesn't mean the end of opportunity for you, our readers. In fact, it has meant the opposite for many brands. A new phenomenon is sweeping the landscape: the 25 million U.S. households that constitute the most affluent segment of the middle market are changing their purchasing patterns. They are making different choices about what goods and services are important, what constitutes quality, and what they will spend their hard-earned dollars on. As a result, they are trading both up and down. Shoppers will pay a premium for the highest quality, remain loyal to those brands, and recommend them to others. But when it comes to commodities, they will look for bargains. It's the Costco phenomenon across a wide and deep palette.

Consumers are looking at each purchase and asking three questions:

1. Is it worth the price premium over a private-label product or one of lesser quality?

2. Does it deliver authenticity and value?

3. When I use this product or service, does it make a statement to my peers about my taste, lifestyle, knowledge, or sense of adventure? Does it make me feel better in a troubled and troubling world?

Companies are responding by turning commodities into luxuries or by creating "masstige" products—affordable versions of superpremium goods. When retailers and manufacturers offer genuine functional and emotional benefits, they move off the old price-demand curve and achieve high profits *and* high-volume sales. Often, it is an industry outsider that has captivated consumers by fundamentally redefining the category. Brands following this new pattern of success include Victoria's Secret lingerie, Starbucks coffee, Crest Whitestrips tooth whiteners, Panera Bread, BMW automobiles, Williams-Sonoma housewares, Kraft's DiGiorno pizza, Ben and Jerry's ice cream, Belvedere Vodka, Diamond Pet Foods, American Girl dolls, and Sub-Zero, Viking, and Whirlpool appliances.

Rapid Adoption

The rise of the "new luxury" is a stark acceleration of a historical phenomenon. Luxury features and technologies have always trickled down as innovations, which are usually introduced at the high end of the market, become more affordable and more widely available over time. But now the quality, taste, and sophistication of luxury products are cascading downmarket faster than ever before. Producers are driving the trend more explicitly and consciously. And consumers are embracing it more eagerly. We call it "the democratization of luxury," and we expect it to retain its potency for a decade to come.

Six forces are driving the phenomenon.

First, new-luxury players are supported by a significant shift in age, marital, income, family, and housing demographics: consumers are marrying later and have more disposable income, fewer children, wealthier parents, and bigger houses than consumers in previous generations. Over the past 50 years, the size of the typical home has more than doubled. And high-tech amenities, such as high-speed data access, are expected to become ubiquitous in U.S. households over the next decade. (See Exhibits 1 and 2.)

Today 1.3 million households in the United States earn more than $400,000 and account for 14 percent of all discretionary spending. Approximately 12 million households earn more than $100,000 and account for half of discretionary spending. Women have been the primary force behind the growth in household income. Approximately 77 percent of married women with children work today. They contribute 33 percent of household income, and roughly 24 percent of them earn more than their spouses. Women are taking the reins on spending, making decisions about items for the home and for themselves, and services that help leverage their time.

Second, the capital markets have been responsive to entrepreneurs with winning ideas. Venture capital firms specializing in consumer products and new retail ideas have helped turn tested concepts into businesses. The entrepreneur with an idea, a prototype, and energy has been empowered with capital.

Third, media role models are reinforcing and legitimizing purchases that help consumers live and feel better. Consider Oprah Winfrey, a leader in the treat-yourself-well movement. Her popular magazine, *O*, and her syndicated talk show have an extraordinarily loyal following. She tells her fans to enjoy their lives, take care of themselves, and spend on indulgences because "you're worth it." They hear her call and spend to her recommendations.

Fourth, consumers can get more information in a shorter amount of time. New products quickly become recognized and enjoy high rates of trial. Word-of-mouth endorsements follow, and retail sales soar.

Exhibit 1	**New Homes Have Become Bigger, Better, and More Affordable**		
	1900	**1950**	**2000**
Total number of housing units in the United States	16 million 60% rural, 40% nonrural	43 million 36% rural, 64% nonrural	107 million 24% rural, 76% nonrural
Typical new home	700 to 1,200 square feet, 0 to 1 bathroom	1,000 square feet, 2 bedrooms, 1 bathroom	2,265 square feet, 3 or more bedrooms, 2 bathrooms, garage for 2 or more cars, central air conditioning, fireplace
Typical financing	Cash (long-term amortized loans not available)	FHA mortgage rate around 4.25%, limited number of financing options	Interest rates around 8% for 30-year mortgage, large selection of financing options
Homeownership rate	46.5%	55.0%	67.4%

SOURCE: National Association of Home Builders, *Housing Facts, Figures and Trends 2001.*

Exhibit 2

By 2010, New Homes Will Have More Amenities

Homes will be similar in size but on smaller lots...	...and with more, smarter amenities
• 2,200 square feet	• Universal design to allow aging at home (master bedroom and laundry on main level)
• 3 or more bedrooms	
• 3 bathrooms	• More efficient heating and cooling systems (two-zone systems)
• Garage for 2 or more cars	
• Average lot size: 1,000 square feet smaller than today's average lot	• More flexible spaces (convertible to home office)
	• Modular wiring systems
• Neighborhoods with narrower streets and fewer paved areas	• High-speed data access
• More mixed-use communities and "new" traditional designs	• More factory-built components (reducing on-site labor costs)
	• More engineered-wood products
• Average sale price: $207,000 to $305,000	• Increased use of steel, concrete, and recycled products
	• More materials and products that require less maintenance
	• More security systems, telephone lines, energy-management systems, and lighting-control systems

SOURCE: National Association of Home Builders, *Housing Facts, Figures and Trends 2001.*

Fifth, consumers are trading down in order to have the funds to trade up—a practice we call "rocketing." Using quality and value as their guides, they seek out less expensive products and services in categories that aren't as important to them. They are more selective about their spending in general and prefer to purchase their core goods from retailers they know and trust. They are particularly interested in reliable products that provide a sense of security and enhance their self-image.

Sixth, today's consumers change partners and jobs more frequently. Between 1961 and 1996, the probability that a marriage would end in divorce increased from 32 percent to 52 percent. Between 1975 and 1996, the likelihood of a second divorce for remarried women increased from 44 percent to 58 percent. The average adult has between 9 and 12 intimate relationships during a lifetime and 13 full-time jobs with different employers. Change fosters spending. During such transitions, people often seek to "reinvent" themselves with new clothes, furniture, homes, cars, and even an improved physical appearance—engineered with cosmetic surgery. (See Exhibit 3.)

Exhibit 3

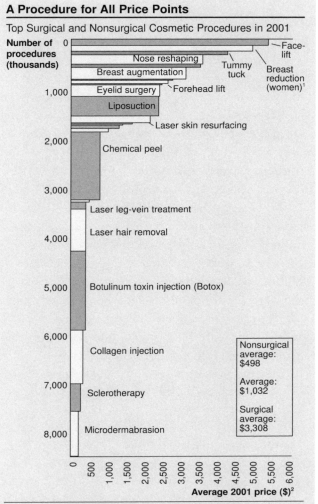

A Procedure for All Price Points

Top Surgical and Nonsurgical Cosmetic Procedures in 2001

SOURCES: American Society for Aesthetic Plastic Surgery 2001 statistical report; BCG analysis.

[1]Breast reduction may be covered by insurance.

[2]Prices reflect only physicians' and surgeons' fees. They do not include fees for the surgical facility, anesthesia, or other costs related to surgery. Figures for procedures often performed on more than one site in the same session (such as Botox injections) reflect typical fees for one site.

Climbing on the Brand Bandwagon

These forces have combined to produce a huge market of consumers who seek to enrich their lives through purchases and consider brands to be crucial for defining themselves and making themselves more attractive. They want to trade up in many categories even if it means they must trade down in others. But whether going upmarket or down-market, these consumers reject mass-market products that *look* as if they were intended for the masses: inexpensive but of poor value, convenient but rarely rewarding, and inoffensive but hardly distinctive or exciting.

Consumers have an exquisitely sensitive built-in calculator that enables them to assess goods and determine if the price is aligned with the value, and how the cost fits into their structure of emotional needs and purchasing power. Consumers no longer believe that expensive automatically means better. They will make a purchase at a price point that their calculators tell them is too high, but only if that product delivers a very potent emotional benefit. They will also buy when their price-value calculators tell them that the price point is very low and they are getting a bargain. Either kind of purchase can provide a significant "shopping rush"—an excitement so real it can actually be measured in a quickened pulse and shallow breathing.

Consider two very different products that are prime examples of the new luxury: BMW automobiles and American Girl dolls. Both sell to the premium segment, and both lay claim to the following:

- The highest loyalty and repurchase rates in their industries

- Controlled retail execution

- Mythic marketing

- A continuous stream of innovations to excite their audience

- Significant price premiums that cover the cost of the best materials and components

Escaping the Average in a BMW

BMW manages the technical-, functional-, and emotional-benefits ladder particularly well. It was founded as an aviation engine company, replacing slow and not-so-dependable Daimler engines on Fokker fighters during World War I. From the time they were installed late in the war, the engines were the most dependable in aviation, and they allowed pilots to go higher and dive faster. That is the heritage on which BMW rests, and it is evident in all aspects of the company's strategy.

Today BMW, the producer of the "ultimate driving machine," is the most profitable car company in the world. A board member puts it this way: "BMW produces *premium* cars, not luxury cars, and they are engineered by people who love cars. Other car companies concentrate on 'visible' features. We make the best vehicle. We are the advocates for drivers. We invented antilock brakes and traction control. A five-year-old BMW still looks new. We have a design that lasts."

Coming from aviation and then motorcycles, BMW entered the performance automobile business as an outsider and has never followed the established rules of car marketing. The company focuses on loyalty, repurchase rates, quality improvements, and cutting-edge innovations in automotive engineering. BMWs are built on the pure aesthetics of speed and driving.

BMW's chief marketing officer describes the company's target customers as people "who work hard and play hard. They treat fun seriously. They enjoy driving. They have high personal energy. Quality is very important, and they are prepared to pay more. Sometimes they don't even take the most direct route to work if there is a better road for driving. They feel completely at peace—protected and invigorated in their driving environment. They are far more likely to wash their cars than other people in the same income cohort. One of the company's management maxims is that it is the customer who decides on the quality of our work. The customer decides on BMW's right to exist."

BMW emphasizes authenticity and stays true to the brand's core ethos. The company operates by strict design principles, which require the very best components, and incorporates substantial innovations and improvements into every redesign. The cars are the most expensive in their product segments and therefore sell at premiums. But they are not about luxury. Their allure starts with the engine, which has the most intricate design and the most power in its class.

Ted, a reconstructive surgeon in Dallas, is a typical new-luxury consumer and the kind of buyer BMW attracts. Ted's wife is also a physician, and they have two children. Ted bought his first BMW—a champagne 7 Series with a tan interior—in 1996. "First we looked at a Lexus," Ted explained. "But in the test drive, the salesperson drove it 20 miles an hour. Then we went to a BMW dealer and got a salesperson who used to sell cars for Lexus and Mercedes. She knew that she was selling a hot car with power. My wife went for a test drive, and she came back with her hair standing up. The car was a kick. It seemed as if it were airborne. She was on highway access roads doing 80 miles an hour and coming to a screeching stop. The brakes never failed. It was like being at Six Flags on a roller coaster, only better. I now have had four BMWs and I'll never ever drive anything else."

The new 7 Series is a good example of BMW's design advantage. It offers an "intelligent" safety and information system, 20-way adjustable seats, active roll stabilization, "stepless" electronic damping control, park-distance control, a six-speed automatic transmission, tire-pressure monitoring, adaptive lights that increase visibility during hard braking, break-resistant security glass, voice-activated navigation, and rain-sensing wipers with a heated fluid supply. It also offers a microfilter ventilation system, hill descent control, and a mayday system that automatically opens a direct line to a live person for roadside assistance. In the past decade, BMW was first to introduce corner brake control, advanced side-airbag protection, and rollover protection. The engine on the 7 Series is a 4.4-liter V-8, which delivers 325 horsepower with acceleration from zero to 60 miles per hour in just 5.9 seconds.

At the other end of the market, BMW recently reintroduced the Mini Cooper with tremendous initial success. The Mini is an old idea with a new twist, brought back to life through a separate division and a new branding approach and distribution system. It is a powerful combination of bold design, performance features, and iconoclastic branding at an accessible price point: the list price is $19,850. Standard amenities in the Cooper S include a six-speed 163-horsepower engine, a six-speaker CD stereo, air conditioning, and six airbags.

The tag line for this remarkable car is "Live me, dress me, protect me, drive me." Buyers get to customize their Minis with colors such as chili red, velvet red, silk green, and pepper white. Options include park-distance control, rain-sensing wipers, performance tires, and a panoramic sunroof. An automotive expert says, "Pound for pound, inch for inch, there's more fun and charm packed into the diminutive 2002 Mini than there is in any other car on the market." Or, as BMW claims in its new ad, "Small is the new black."

Through clever segmentation and maniacal adherence to its core identity, BMW has extended its position in the premium segment. In last year's down economy, BMW automobile deliveries grew 10 percent. This year, the company will again see double-digit growth and substantial share gain. BMW has managed to make its brands both more accessible and more aspirational, with a top price that is nearly seven times its lowest.

BMW drivers aren't just owners; they are apostles who hear the engine, feel the road, and *experience* the drive. They love their cars. Here's how BMW customers describe it: "The car drives like a dream." "The car and I are one." "My car sees the curves and smiles." "I feel like a cheetah."

Entertainment and Education: A Mother's Dream

Many of the most successful new-luxury brands are born in frustration—usually when the future founder of the brand directly experiences the compromises forced on consumers by standard products. Pleasant Rowland, a former elementary-school teacher and writer of educational materials, wanted to buy her niece a doll, but she didn't like the Barbie and Cabbage Patch offerings that dominated the shelves of toy stores everywhere. She objected to the materials, components, and design of these mass-market products, not to mention their lack of educational value.

So Rowland started a company to produce something better, but it doesn't consider itself to be a doll company. Rather, American Girl sells history, education, entertainment, empowerment, authenticity, and imagination all wrapped up in top-quality workmanship and materials. The doll collection features eight characters from various eras, from its newest creation, Kaya, a Native American girl of the Nez Perce tribe living in 1764, to Molly, a World War II–era girl in the Midwest. Books about the characters and historically accurate accessories—clothes, furniture, and toys—provide a tangible piece of history.

Samantha, an eight-year-old fan of American Girl dolls, told us that her doll, also named Samantha, is her best friend. The Samantha doll is American Girl's number one seller. This character is a nine-year-old orphan living with her grandmother in New York City at the beginning of the twentieth century. American Girl offers six volumes of stories about Samantha, so Samantha (the girl) knows where her friend grew up and how she made it through tough times. "I love to dress her and care for her. I even have clothes that match hers so that we can dress alike." One day, Samantha (the doll) was injured when the girl's brother tossed her out a window. Samantha's mother called American Girl and was told to return the doll to the company for repairs. She came back as good as new from the "doll hospital" after being treated by a "doctor." She even had a hospital bracelet on her wrist.

Word-of-Mother Marketing

Samantha's mother found out about American Girl from the mother of her daughter's friend. Now she tells her friends to "buy the doll that comes with a history lesson." "If you want your child to read and to have perspective on her place in the world," she explains, "then get her an American Girl doll and the books that go with it." That's word-of-mother marketing.

American Girl dolls cost around $85—a 400-to-800-percent premium over the most popular dolls. But many mothers feel that providing their daughters with a wholesome, inviting way to learn through fantasy about heroines that prospered under difficult conditions is worth that price. The brand commands extraordinary loyalty, and girls clamor for the continuous stream of product extensions that build on the original idea (including a monthly magazine with a circulation of 650,000). With return rates of less than 2 percent, the company has a lot of satisfied customers. Today American Girl has the highest-performing retail store on Chicago's Michigan Avenue. The company generates annual revenues of $370 million and continues to grow at double-digit rates.

Shattering Conventions

The new luxury is not a marketing strategy but a whole new way of looking at business and the world. And it has shattered conventions in most aspects of marketing and branding, including assumptions about price ceilings, price ranges, brand extendibility, consumer sophistication, market stability, and the time it takes luxury to cascade to the middle market. New strategies are required to win in this game. Here are seven practices that a new-luxury player can follow to transform a category or brand.

1. **Don't underestimate the consumer.** Consumers will trade up to higher levels of quality, taste, and aspiration if the benefits are worth it.

2. **Move off the demand curve, not along it.** With a bold vision, you can price up, spend back, and reap disproportionate profits.

3. **Create a technical-, functional-, and emotional-benefits ladder.** Offer functional advantages that are tied to targeted emotions as well as a technical platform that lends credibility to functional claims. If your strategy is well executed, consumers will ladder from technical to functional to emotional benefits, responding so powerfully that you can break through the traditional price barriers by creating greater demand.

4. **Escalate innovation, elevate quality, and deliver a flawless experience.**
    Technical and functional advantages are short-lived. The quality bar
    is rising at all price points.

5. **Stretch the brand over a broader price range with increasingly pre-
    cise segmentation.** New-luxury players often have a five- to tenfold
    spread between their highest and lowest price points. They take the
    brand upmarket for aspirational appeal and extend it down-market
    to make it more accessible and competitive.

6. **Create and own brand apostles.** Heavy users drive volume and
    spread the word. In categories of frequently purchased goods, the
    top 10 percent of customers generate up to half of the category's
    sales and profits.

7. **Attack your category as if you were an outsider.** Since outsiders typ-
    ically generate most of the disruptive innovations, incumbents must
    find a way to break the pattern by creating their own innovations.

*   *   *

For established competitors, especially those targeting middle-market
consumers with midlevel products, the new luxury can be an opportunity or
a threat. Meeting the challenge will require a new frame of reference and a
different kind of leadership: more imagination and less dogma, more
courage and less convention, more creativity and less incrementalism. When
facing a new-luxury rival that enters the market at a tremendous price dif-
ferential, many executives will declare, "There can't be enough volume at
that price point!" But there can be if the product offers the right combination of technical, functional, and emotional benefits. The democratization
of luxury gives imaginative leaders a new way to think about growth, profitability, and the art of fulfilling dreams.

In an uncertain economy, it takes courage to pursue a trading-up strategy. In the face of softening category demand and pricing pressure, many
brand managers are undoubtedly looking at ways to trim a few pennies from
their product costs in order to protect margins. Either by choice or by fate,
they will trade their customers down.

Those with vision and leadership will take a different route. They will
ask: "How can I invest *more* in product quality and design? How can I
strengthen my opening price position while extending my brand upmarket?